World Showc

MW00487399

Table of Contents

Dining in the World Showcase

At Epcot you can travel around the world, under the sea, into outer space... and beyond all in one place!

At Epcot Center, as it was originally called, you can see the whole world in just one day. Plus, you can see how technology has changed the world and how it will impact the world in the future.

There are two "Worlds" at Epcot. They are called Future World and the World Showcase. The two "Worlds" don't seem to have a lot in common, but together, they make one great theme park.

THE 2 WORLDS

Epcot is divided into 2 worlds. Future World which looks at technology and the future, and the World Showcase which highlights countries from around the real world showcases the culture and cuisine from these various countries.

FUTURE WORLD

Future World looks at the future of the world. Each of the pavilions in Future World showcase a different technology that is prevalent in our world today. From The Seas, all the way around to Test Track, technology and innovation are on display.

Future World has evolved over the years from the slightly boring exhibits that Epcot Center started with. Now, with the addition of Soarin', Mission Space and Nemo, this park is really a great place to spend the day.

There are eight active pavilions in Future World. They are centered around the big, main pavilion which is called Innoventions. It's not near as beautiful as Cinderella Castle, but is functional as the Center of Epcot Future World.

Here is a list of the pavilions with the attractions in each

The Seas with Nemo and Friends

Sea Base Alpha

Turtle Talk - Starring Crush
The Manatee Exhibit

The Land
Soarin'
Living with the Land
The Circle of Life

Journey to Imagination
Captain EO
Journey to Imagination starring Figment

Future World
Test Track
Mission Space
Universe of Energy
Spaceship Earth
Innoventions

Some of the best and most thrilling rides anywhere can be found in Future World. You could spend a whole day in this part of the park and not see everything. It's not to be missed.

The attractions in Future World are some of the most innovative in all of Walt Disney World. Test Track and Mission Space have some mind-blowing technology and Soarin' may be the most popular ride in the park.

Dining in Future World

Fine Dining is really not what Future World is known for. For really good food, you have to go across the lagoon.

Here are the restaurants you'll find in Future World -

In The Seas - Coral Reef Restaurant

In the Land - Sunshine Seasons Food Court and the Garden Grill

In Innoventions - Electric Umbrella

If you are into fine cuisine from around the world, then WORLD SHOWCASE is where you want to be.

Epcot's World Showcase is Disney's tribute to the concept of a World's Fair. It has food from a number of different countries and cultures. Each of the countries is staffed by cast members from the country, which brings a real authenticity to the experience. There are 11 World Showcase Pavilions. 10 of these are the original pavilions from when the park first opened October 1st, 1982. Norway was added later in 1988. For over 30 years the World Showcase has stayed the same while the other side of Epcot has changed considerably.

The World Showcase, unlike most of the other parks, is not about the rides. It's about showcasing other parts of the world. Each country brings the best it has to offer in food, goods and entertainment to share with the world.

The attractions in the World Showcase aren't the stars of the show. The World Showcase is all about the best of each country. Each pavilion is full of authentic items from each country. It really is something special.

The World Showcase

If you are going to eat in Epcot, this is the place to do it. Dining is the star of the World Showcase. Some of the best restaurants in the whole world are located here. Each country has at least one Table Service restaurant and one Quick Service restaurant.

Mexico - San Angel Inn, La Cava del Tequila, La Hacienda y La Cantina (outside)

Norway - Akershus Royal Banquet Hall, Kringla Bakeri og Kafe

China - Nine Dragons, Lotus Blossom Cafe

Germany - Biergarten

Italy - Via Napoli, Tutto Italia

America - Liberty Inn

Japan - Teppan Edo, Katsura Grill, Tokyo Dining

Morocco - Restaurant Marrakesh, Tangerine Cafe

France - Chefs de France, Bistro de Paris, Boulangerie Paitisserie

United Kingdom - Rose and Crown, Yorkshire County Fish Shop

Canada - Le Cellier

· The hardest part of eating at Epcot's World Showcase is leaving and knowing that you may never get to taste this quality of food again.

But don't worry. We put this amazing cookbook together so that you can experience the cousins of The World Showcase right in your own home.

The Mexico Pavilion

The Epcot Mexico Pavilion is the first pavilion you reach when you enter the World Showcase to the left of Spaceship Earth (the big silver ball), or on the Test Track side of Epcot. Many visitors say that it is also the most beautiful of the pavilions in the World Showcase.

There is only one building in this area. It's the big pyramid with all the steps. This makes this area unique in the World Showcase. The other pavilions have more than one building, but here everything is housed inside the big pyramid.

The Food

There is really only one restaurant in Mexico, but it has three parts, two inside and one outside.

San Angel Inn

Inside the pyramid you will find the San Angel Inn. It's a Mexican food restaurant that serves authentic dishes, and not an Americanized version. It's based on a restaurant found in Mexico City that's been around for almost 100 years.

La Cava de Tequila

There is also La Cava de Tequila (the cave of Tequila), a 30 seat restaurant tucked back inside a cave. It serves some potent drinks (over 70 types of Tequila are available) and tapas with great toppings.

La Hacienda y La Cantina

La Hacienda y La Cantina are the new restaurants in Mexico. They are located right outside the Epcot Mexico Pavilion on the World Showcase Lagoon; this dining attraction is perfect for those looking for authentic Mexican cuisine or just something quick.

La Hacienda is the sit down portion of the restaurant. It has seating both inside and outside. La Cantina is the quick service restaurant that has to go Mexican Food with outside seating.

Classic Margarita

2 parts tequila
1 part Cointreau
2 parts lime juice
1 part simple syrup made with agave nectar
Shake and serve in the salt rimmed glass over ice

Midnight Blue Patron Margarita

2 parts Patron tequila
1 part blue curacao
2 parts sweet and sour mix
1 part simple syrup
splash of Rose's Lime Juice
Blend with ice and serve in a salt rimmed glass

Mango Margarita

2 parts tequila
1 part triple sec
2 parts sweet and sour mix
1 part frozen mango in syrup or Monin or Island Oasis mango
puree
splash of Rose's Lime Juice
Blend with ice and serve in a salt rimmed glass

Strawberry Margarita

2 parts tequila
1 part triple sec
2 parts sweet and sour mix
1 part frozen strawberries in syrup or Monin or Island Oasis
strawberry puree
Blend with ice and serve in a salt rimmed glass

Lime Margarita

2 parts tequila
1 part triple sec
2 parts sweet and sour mix
1 part simple syrup
a good squeeze of Rose's lime juice - maybe a little less than 1 part
Blend with ice and serve in a salt rimmed glass

Pineapple Margarita

2 parts tequila

1 part ginger liquor

1 part pineapple juice - simmered down to a syrup consistency until
it is reduced to half of what you started with.

1 part lime juice

1 part simple syrup made with agave nectar

Shake and serve in the salt rimmed glass over ice

Blood Orange Margarita

2 parts white tequila
1 part triple sec
1 part lime juice
1 part hibiscus syrup
1 part blood orange juice
Shake and serve in the salt rimmed glass over ice and top with blood
orange foam

Prickly Pear Margarita

2 parts white tequila
1 part triple sec
1 part Monin or Island Oasis prickly pear puree
1 part lime juice
1 part simple syrup made with agave nectar
Shake and serve in the salt rimmed glass over ice

Passion Fruit Margarita

2 parts tequila
1 part ginger liquor
1/2 part Monin or Island Oasis passion fruit puree
1/2 part Monin or Island Oasis mango puree, 1 part lime juice
1 part simple syrup made with agave nectar.
Shake and serve in the salt rimmed glass over ice

Cucumber Margarita

1/3 of one fresh cucumber peeled and seeded and then cut into about 1 1/2 inch pieces.
About a 2 inch piece of a green bell pepper, seeded.
1 part triple sec
1 part pineapple juice
1 part simple syrup made with agave nectar
Place the fruit in the bottom of your glass and muddle to release some of the juices. Don't go crazy here, muddling shouldn't create a mush of the fruit, just sufficiently bruise them.
Now top off the glass with ice and add 2 parts tequila, 1 part triple sec, 1 part pineapple juice - which has been simmered down to a syrup, 1 part simple syrup made with agave nectar. Shake and serve in a salt rimmed glass.

La Cava Margarita

2 parts tequila
1 part triple sec
2 parts lime juice
1 part simple syrup made with agave nectar
Shake and serve in the salt rimmed glass over ice

Avocado Margarita

Place about 1/3 of a very ripe avocado in a blender. Top with ice (*measured with the glass you're going to be serving in*) and add 2 parts tequila, 1 part Midori liqueur, 2 parts lime juice, 1 part simple syrup made with agave nectar.
Blend until smooth and serve in a salt rimmed glass.

Jalapeno Margarita

1/4 of one fresh cucumber peeled and seeded and then cut into 1 1/2 inch pieces

2 inch piece of a green bell pepper, seeded

1/2 of 1 small jalapeno seeded and cut into 1 1/2 inch pieces.

Place the fruit in the bottom of your glass and muddle to release some of the juices. Don't go crazy here, muddling shouldn't create a mush of the fruit, just sufficiently bruise them. Now top off the glass with ice and add 2 parts tequila, 1 part triple sec, 2 parts lime juice, 1 part simple syrup made with agave nectar.

Shake and serve in a salt rimmed glass.

Conga Juice

5 cups orange juice (*pulp free*)
2 cups pineapple juice
1/2 cup lime juice
1/4 cup Maraschino cherry juice
Best served over crushed ice, or put in freezer to create a slush type drink

Tequila Sangrita

Makes 1 gallon
24 oz. tomato juice
6 serrano peppers, very fine chopped
half of a red onion, very fine chopped
17 mint leaves, very fine chopped
7 oz. fresh lime juice
7 oz. fresh grapefruit juice
7 oz. fresh orange juice
salt to taste
This salsa-like chaser follows a tequila shot at La Cava del Tequila
Mix all the ingredients together and shake well

House Ranch Dressing

1/2 Cup Mayonnaise
1/4 Cup Sour Cream
1/4 Cup Buttermilk
1/2tsp. Worcestershire sauce
1tsp. Lemon Juice
1 tsp. White Vinegar
1 tsp. Freshly Minced Garlic
1/2 tsp. Salt
1 tsp. Sugar
1/8 tsp. Cumin
1/8 tsp. Pepper
1/8 tsp. Tarragon
1/8 tsp. Oregano
1/8 tsp. Basil
1 tsp. Fresh Parsley (*chopped*)
1 tsp. Chipotle Pepper (*chopped*)
1Tbs Cilantro
Milk (*as needed*)

For dressing, combine all liquid ingredients in a bowl,
whipping at medium speed until smooth
Add dry ingredients and mix well (you may add milk to obtain
desired texture).
Refrigerate until ready to serve.

Ensalada de la Casa

Yield: 4 servings

Salad:

12 ounces green lettuce mix
1 small jicama, peeled and cut into strips
1 small can of cactus strips
1/2 lb. cherry tomatoes, cut in half
1/2 of a small red onion, cut into slices
1/2 of a red bell pepper, cut into slices
1/4 cup shredded Monterey Jack cheese
1 avocado, peeled and cut into slices

House Ranch Dressing

1/2 cup mayonnaise
1/4 cup each: sour cream and buttermilk
1/2 teaspoon Worcestershire sauce
1 teaspoon each: lemon juice, white vinegar and freshly minced garlic
1/2 teaspoon salt
1 teaspoon sugar
1/8 teaspoon each: ground cumin, pepper, tarragon, ground oregano and ground basil
1 teaspoon each chopped: fresh parsley and chipotle pepper
3 teaspoons cilantro
milk as needed

For dressing, combine all liquid ingredients in a bowl, whipping at medium speed until smooth. Add dry ingredients and mix well (*you may add milk to obtain desired texture*).

Refrigerate until ready to serve.

In bowl, toss salad ingredients. Add dressing to taste.

Note: Chipotle peppers are dried, smoked jalapeños.
Chipotles are sold dried, pickled and canned in adobo sauce.

Sopa Azteca

Yield: 4 Servings

3 tablespoon olive oil, divided
1/3 cup onion, chopped
1 1/3 cups tomatoes, peeled, seeded and chopped
1 teaspoon garlic
1 quart chicken broth
2 tablespoons dill
2 whole fresh red chili peppers
4 soft corn tortillas
1/2 cup ripe avocado, cubed
4 tablespoons sour cream
1/4 cup Monterey Jack Cheese, shredded

Heat 2 tablespoons of oil in a large saucepan.
Sauté' onion, tomatoes, and garlic until tender *(5 minutes)*.
Add chicken broth and dill.
Cover and simmer for 20 minutes.
Remove seeds and stems from peppers and cut each in 2 pieces lengthwise.
Cut tortillas in 1/3 inch strips and set aside.
Heat the remaining tablespoon of oil in small skillet and sauté peppers for 1 to 2 minutes.
Remove and drain on paper towel.
Add tortilla strips and cook until golden brown.
Remove and drain separately on paper towel.
Divide peppers, tortilla strips and avocado among 4 heavy bowls.
Pour hot chicken broth into bowls.
Garnish with sour cream and Monterey Jack cheese.

Sopa De Elote
(Corn Chowder)

Yield: 6 servings

1 1/2 pounds corn (*off the co*b)

3 ounces flour

4 ounces onions, diced

3 ounces poblano pepper, skinned seeded & diced

4 ounces butter

1 1/2 quart half & half cream

1/2 ounce garlic, diced

salt to taste

In a medium size pot, melt butter over medium heat and slowly add the flour.

Then add the garlic and the diced onions.

When blended together, add only 1qt. of the half & half, and 1 lb. of the corn

When the mixture thickens, add the remaining corn and half & half, salt to taste.

Then add the Poblano Peppers.

Salsa Ranchera

1lb Tomatillos (*remove outer shell*)
1½lb Tomatoes
1 Clove Garlic (*minced*)
4oz Chorizo (*cooked & chopped*)
1½oz Flour
1/2 Cup Olive Oil
2oz Chile Chipotle (*chopped*)
1tsp Salt
¼tsp Black pepper
½tsp Sugar
3 Cups Water
4- 6oz Beef Tenderloins
4 Corn Tortillas

On a hot grill proceed to roast the garlic, tomatillos and tomatoes
Then remove and place in blender together with the water, salt,
black pepper and sugar
In a medium stock pot add olive oil, when oil is hot add flour, diced
onions, chipotle pepper, chorizo and the "salsa" from the blender.
Bring to a boil
reduce heat. Cook until salsa thickens
Place beef tenderloins on a hot grill and cook to desire tenderness,
and then remove from stove
Take corn tortillas and dip them quickly in hot oil, remove (this is
done to soften tortillas)
Place one corn tortilla on a plate
Place the beef tenderloin on top of the tortilla and cover with the
salsa.

Beef Ranchera

Yield: 4 servings
Salsa Ranchera:
1 pound tomatillos (*remove outer shell*)
1 1/2 pounds tomatoes
1/2 ounce garlic
4 ounces chorizo, cooked & chopped
1 1/2 ounces flour
2 ounces cilantro, chopped
4 ounces diced Spanish onions
4 ounces olive oil
2 ounces Chile chipotle, chopped
0.7 ounce salt
1/4 teaspoon black pepper
1/2 teaspoon sugar
24 ounces water
Beef Tenderloin
4 (6 oz.) beef tenderloins
4 corn tortillas

On a hot grill proceed to roast the garlic, tomatillos and tomatoes.
Then remove and place in blender together with the water, salt,
black pepper and sugar.
In a medium stock pot add olive oil, when oil is hot add flour, diced
onions, chipotle pepper, chorizo and the "salsa" from the blender.
Bring to a boil, and then reduce heat. Cook until salsa thickens.
Place beef tenderloins on a hot grill and cook to desire tenderness,
and then remove from stove.
Take corn tortillas and dip them quickly in hot oil, then remove
(*this is done to soften tortillas*)
Place one corn tortilla on a plate.

Place the beef tenderloin on top of the tortilla and cover with the salsa.

Tostadas de Tinga

Pulled chicken seasoned with roasted tomato and chipotle,
served on tostadas with black refried beans, guacamole and sour
cream

Marinated Chicken:
8 ounces chicken breast
1/2 ounce diced onions
4 garlic cloves, chopped
16 ounces water
3 ounces chipotle paste
3 ounces tomato puree
salt and pepper to taste

Tostadas
8 ounces cooked chicken (*see above*)
4 small corn tostadas (*or corn tortillas, cut with a round cutter to
slightly larger than chip size*)
4 ounces refried black beans, warmed
2 ounces Queso fresco or shredded Monterey Jack cheese
1 ounce guacamole
2 ounces sour cream

In a large pot with water, boil chicken.
Once cooked, cool down the chicken and shred. Set aside.
Sauté onions in a saucepan until they are caramelized and then dd
garlic.
Add water, chipotle paste, tomato puree, and chicken.
Cook over medium for 30 to 40 minutes and salt to taste.
In a sauté pan with a thin layer or oil,

fry corn tortillas until crunchy (*step not needed if using small tostadas*).

Allow to drain on paper towels.

To assemble: spread layer of warmed refried black beans on tostada.

Add shredded, cooked, marinated chicken.

Top with drizzle of guacamole, sour cream, and top with cheese.

Serve immediately.

Nachos Del Pollo y Chorizo

Yield: 4 servings.

1 1/2 pounds chicken breast strips
1/2 teaspoon minced garlic
1/2 teaspoon salt
1/2 teaspoon black pepper
1 pound peeled, diced, cooked chorizo
10 cups corn chips
6 cups shredded Monterey Jack cheese
1 1/2 cups diced tomatoes
1 cup sliced jalapeño peppers
1 cup sour cream

Red Sauce

8 ounces tomatoes, canned
2 tablespoon chopped white onion
1 garlic clove
to taste salt

Heat oven to 350 degrees
Season chicken breast strips with garlic, salt and black pepper.
Lightly coat a heavy skillet with cooking spray.
Cook chicken in skillet until meat is no longer pink in the center.
For the sauce, in a blender, combine the canned of tomatoes, onion and garlic clove.
Blend all until puréed. Place mixture in a saucepan and bring to a boil.
Add salt to taste; set aside.
Place the corn chips on oven-safe baking dish.
Add the cooked chicken strips and chorizo on top of the corn chips
Cover with the shredded cheese. Place in oven, uncovered, for 5 minutes or until cheese is melted.

Remove from the oven and top with diced tomatoes, jalapeño peppers and sour cream.
Add red sauce on top to taste.

Pollo A Las Rajas

Yield: 4 servings

4 chicken breast halves

1 cup of chorizo, casing removed and diced

1 large red bell pepper

1 large Spanish onion

1 large Poblano chili

1 garlic clove, chopped

1/4 teaspoon ground black pepper

5 tablespoons vegetable oil

1 cup sour cream

1 cup Monterey Jack cheese, shredded

1/2 cup half-and-half cream

Season the chicken breast halves with garlic, salt, and black pepper.
Place the chicken breast halves in a roasting pan and bake in the
oven at 350 for 20 minutes or until cooked.

In a saucepan heat 2 tablespoons of oil and lightly sauté Poblano
pepper until skin starts separating.

Peel skin from Poblano pepper.

Make a slit and remove all the seeds. Slice onion, bell pepper, and
Poblano pepper into strips.

In a heavy skillet heat remaining 3 tablespoons of oil and add
chorizo, garlic, onion, and peppers.

Cook over medium high heat stirring occasionally until onions and
peppers are soft.

Add sour cream, half-and-half, black pepper and salt and simmer for
three minutes.

On ovenproof serving dishes, place 3/4 cup of vegetable mixture.
Top with roasted chicken breast.

Sprinkle 1/4 cup Monterey Jack cheese on each serving plate.
Broil until cheese melts and turns golden.

Serve.

Queso Fundido

Yield: 4 servings

1/2 pound Muenster cheese

1/4 pound chorizo sausage

6 flour tortillas

Slice or grate cheese and set aside.

Peel chorizo sausage and cut into large chunks.

Sauté in a small frying pan until nicely browned.

Break up sausage into small pieces while browning and drain any excess fat.

Lightly grease a shallow oven/broiler-proof casserole dish.

Arrange half the cheese in bottom of the dish.

Top with cooked sausage and remaining cheese.

Broil until cheese melts and lightly browns.

Warm tortillas and cut into quarters.

Spoon melted cheese mixture onto tortilla pieces and serve immediately.

Chiles en Nogada

Yield: 4 servings
Filling
1 pound ground pork meat
1/3 cup onions, diced
2 garlic cloves, chopped
1/2 cup fresh peaches, diced
1/3 cup raisins
1/3 cup walnuts, chopped
1/3 cup almonds, chopped
1/2 teaspoon sugar
2 cloves, chopped
1/2 cup tomato sauce
1/4 tablespoon ground cinnamon
1 tablespoon vegetable oil
1/4 teaspoon salt
1/4 teaspoon ground black pepper
1/2 cup fresh pears, diced

In a frying pan place, one tablespoon of oil.
When the oil is hot add the ground pork meat, onions, garlic first
and then all the rest of the ingredients and cook for 15 minutes.

PREPARATION FOR THE CHILES
Roast the 8 chiles poblanos in a gas burner, then, peel and remove
the burned skin, the seeds and veins of the chiles and rinse them.
Proceed to stuff the chiles with the filling prepared before.

Walnut Sauce:
2 cups walnuts
2 slices white bread
1 cup Mexican fresh cheese
1 cup sour cream
1 teaspoon sugar

1/4 teaspoon ground cinnamon
1/2 teaspoon salt
3 cups Half and Half cream
Place all ingredients in a blender and blend until smooth. Pour cold sauce over the chiles.

The Norway Pavilion

The Epcot Norway Pavilion is the home to a splash of Norwegian culture, some pretty good eats, and a whole lot of Frozen. There's a ride, gift shop and meet-and-greet all in honor of Elsa, Anna, Olaf and the gang. The Princess Storybook (Breakfast, Lunch and Dinner) is hosted at Akershus Royal Banquet Hall and is very popular (but at this time, does not feature Anna and Elsa, so beware).

The pavilion is designed to look like a village in Norway. It includes a replica of a church, called the Stave church. There used to be a full-scale Viking ship, but it was removed years ago.

The Food

There is one sit down restaurant and one great snack food joint in Norway.

The Akershus Royal Banquet Hall is home of the daily Princess Character breakfast, lunch and dinner. This used to be a breakfast only event, but it was incredibly popular and lunch and dinner were added.

Kringla Bakeri og Kafe is a neat snack food joint. A Kringla is a round (like a pretzel) Norwegian pastry.

Tromso

1 part Bailey's Irish Cream
1 part Disaronno Amaretto
2 parts strong coffee (cold)
1 part half & half.
Blend with ice and serve.

Linie Aquavit Glacier Shot

1 part Aquavit
1 part vodka
4 parts Sprite
splash of Rose's Lime juice

Prince of Norway

1 part apricot brandy
1 part sloe gin
1 part sweet and sour mix
2 parts orange juice

The Stavanger

1 part Aquavit
1 part vodka
1 part Monin or Island Oasis raspberry puree or frozen raspberries
in syrup
2 parts sweet and sour mix
Blend with ice and serve.

The Kristiansand

1 part Aquavit

1 part rum

1/2 part each of mango and raspberry puree from Monin or Island Oasis or frozen in syrup

2 parts sweet and sour mix

Blend with ice and serve.

The Oslo

1 part vodka
1/2 part each Aquavit and crème de banana
1 part Monin or Island Oasis strawberry puree or frozen in syrup
2 parts sweet and sour mix
Blend with ice and serve.

Viking Coffee

1 part Kahlua
1 part Bailey's
6 parts good coffee

Atlantic salmon Filet

Yield: 4 servings

4 – 6oz Salmon Filets

4Tbs Tamarind Glaze

2Tbs Wasabi Coulis

2Tbs Pesto

Salt to taste

Pepper to taste

Pre-heat convection oven to 400 degrees

Lay out salmon on a sheet pan, season lightly and coat with
Tamarind Glaze

Bake salmon until internal temperature of 140 degrees is achieved

Drizzle Wasabi Coulis and Pesto over exterior of fish in a crisscross
fashion

Plate and serve

Kjottkaker

1lb Ground Pork
1lb Ground Beef
2oz Shallots (*minced*)
2oz Capers (*minced*)
5oz Beets (*steamed or canned*)
2T Dijon Mustard
Kosher Salt
Pepper
Olive Oil

Steam beets just until knife tender, peel and small dice
Mince all vegetables and mix all ingredients together
Test a small amount for seasoning
Form 1 to 1 ½ ounce portion patties
Pan fry in olive oil to medium well

Breakfast Potato Casserole

1 ½lbs Potatoes (*diced*)
1 ½lbs Potatoes (*shredded*)
4oz White Onions (*diced*)
1 Cup Cheddar Cheese (*shredded, save half for topping*)
1 Cup Jarlsberg Cheese (*shredded*)
1 Cup Sour Cream
Salt
Pepper
1/2 Cup Milk
In mixing bowl combine all ingredients and mix well by hand.
Place in greased casserole or non-stick pan.
Sprinkle with reserved cheese on top.
Cover with waxed paper and then aluminum foil.
Bake in 350-degree oven for approximately 40 minutes.
Remove foil and paper for last 10 minutes to brown top if desired.

Cauliflower Mashed Potatoes

½ Cup Butter
4lbs Red Potatoes
1 Head of Cauliflower
2 Cups Jarlsburg Cheese (*grated*)
1 Cup Heavy Cream
Salt
Pepper
Steam the potatoes until soft
Steam cauliflower in separate pan until soft
Add all ingredients and mix on low speed
Season to taste

Cauliflower Soup with Chive Oil for Garnish

& Sourdough Croutons

Yield: 8 servings
4Tbs Butter
1 large Onion (*diced*)
¼ Cup Shallots (*chopped*)
1/8 Cup Roasted Garlic Puree
4lbs Cauliflower Florets
¼ Cup EJ Brandy
2 2/3 Cup Chicken Stock
5 Cups Heavy Cream
1Tbs Thyme (*chopped*)
Allspice (*to taste*)
Crushed Red Pepper (*to taste*)
Kosher Salt (*to taste*)
Ground White Pepper (*to taste*)
½ Cup Butter

On a cookie sheet, roast the shallots, garlic, onions until tender on
350° degree oven.
When cooled, puree in a blender.
Roast the cauliflower until lightly colored.
In a large soup pot, melt 4 tablespoons of butter.
Add onions and shallots.
Add the florets and allow to slightly brown, stir in garlic puree.
Deglaze the pot with the brandy.

Add chicken stock and cream. Allow the florets to soften until fork
tender.
Puree with a stick blender or in a blender.
Add spices to taste.
Add the remaining butter to finish soup.

Chive Oil for Garnish

1 Cup Chives
1 Cup Olive Oil
In a airtight container, let steep a minimum of 24 hours.
Stain though cheesecloth
Store in airtight container

Sourdough Croutons for Garnish

½ loaf of Sourdough Baguette
Olive Oil (*to lightly coat bread*)
Salt (*to taste*)
Pepper (*to taste*)
Small dice sourdough baguette and place in a bowl.
Lightly toss with oil, salt and pepper.
Place on a cookie pan and cook at 350° until golden brown.

Chicken Salad

2 Cups Cooked Chicken (*diced*)
½ Cup Mushrooms (*sliced, blanched and drained*)
½ Cup Asparagus (*blanched*)

Dressing

¾ Cup Mayonnaise
1 Tbs Lemon Juice
½t Celery Salt
1 Tbs Sweet Pickle Juice
Salt
White Pepper
Place chicken, mushrooms, and asparagus in a mixing bowl.
Mix the ingredients for the dressing and pour over the chicken,
mushrooms, and asparagus.
Mix well.

Christmas Bread

1 quart Milk
7 Tbs Yeast
1 Cup Butter
1 Cup Sugar
1 ½tsp Cardamom
6 Cups Flour
1/2 Cup Raisins
3oz Citron (*chopped*)

Heat milk to lukewarm and stir in the yeast.
Melt margarine and sugar together and add with the remaining
ingredients
to form a medium stiff dough.
Let rise.
Divide the dough into four parts.
Knead and form into loaves.
Let rise again.
Preheat oven to 425° F.
Bake approximately one hour.

Garlic Buttered Broccoli

Yield: 4 servings
1lb Broccoli
½ Red Onion (*thinly sliced*)
½ Red Bell Pepper (*thinly sliced*)
10 Nicoise Olives (*pit removed and quartered*)
1/2 Stick Unsalted Butter
1tsp Garlic (*chopped*)
Cook broccoli to desired doneness in boiling water
shock with ice and water to stop the cooking process.
Melt butter in pre-heated sauté pan and add onion, peppers, olives
and garlic
Toss in broccoli and season to taste

Leek and Jarlsburg Cheese Soup

1 Cup Butter
1 Cup Flour
1 Yellow Onion (*chopped*)
1 large Leek (*washed and chopped into ¼" pieces*)
1/2Tbs Tabasco Sauce
2Tbs Worcestershire Sauce
½Tbs Onion Powder
8oz Jarlsburg Cheese (*or cheese of your choice grated*)
2 Cups Milk
1 Can Chicken Broth
Salt
Pepper
Chives for Garnish
In a large saucepan, melt butter on low heat
Add onions and cook until translucent
Add flour to make a roux
Cook for 5 minutes, stirring
Add cold milk and chicken broth, stirring constantly
Add leeks, onion power, Tabasco and Worcestershire sauce
Cook on medium heat until soup thickens
Add cheese, stirring until melted
Season to taste with salt and pepper
Before serving, add chives for garnish

Mashed Rutabaga

½lb Rutabaga
¼lb Carrots
¼lb Potatoes
1 ½ Cups Half and Half
4Tbs Butter
1Tbs Sugar
Salt to taste
White Pepper to taste
Nutmeg to taste

Place rutabaga, carrots, and potatoes in a pan.
Add water and boil until soft; pour off water.
Bring half and half to a boil, add butter.
Mix the vegetables in the chopper; slowly add the hot mixture of
cream and butter until the rutabaga reaches the right thickness.
Season to taste

Orange-Horse Radish Chicken Salad

1lb Cooked Chicken Breast (*diced*)
1 Stalk Celery (*finely diced*)
½ Red Onion (*finely diced*)
1tsp Worcestershire Sauce
2tsp Horseradish
1 Cup Orange Marmalade
¼ Cup Mayonnaise
Salt
Pepper
Take marmalade, mayonnaise, horseradish, Worcestershire sauce,
celery and onion and mix thoroughly
Add in chicken and coat well
Season to taste and chill

Roasted Mushroom Salad

Yield: 4 servings

1/2 Cup Portobello Mushroom (*destem and cut into 4 pieces*)

1/2 Cup Crimini Mushrooms

1/2 Cup Button Mushrooms

1/4tsp Garlic (*minced*)

1/2 Cup Shallots (*sliced*)

1tsp Kosher Salt

1t Ground Black Pepper

1tsp Garlic Oil

Destem and remove the insides of the Portobello mushrooms. Cut into 4 pieces.

Wash the remaining mushrooms.

Mince the garlic.

Slice the shallots.

Toss all ingredients together.

Roast in oven for 15 minutes at 350 degrees F.

Seafood Chowder

3 Tbs Butter
1 large White Onion (*diced*)
1 Can (16oz) Diced Tomatoes
3 large White Potatoes (*diced*)
4 Cups Heavy Cream
Kosher Salt
Ground black pepper
Tabasco sauce
1 ½ Cup Salmon (*cooked*)
1 Cup Cod (*cooked*)
1 Cup of Small Shrimp (*cooked*)
1 In a large soup pot, heat butter on medium heat
Sauté onions and tomatoes
Add potatoes and heavy cream
Cook until the potatoes are fork tender
Season with salt, pepper and Tabasco sauce
Serve soup with seafood pieces

Princess Cake Sponge Cake

3 Eggs
1 Cup Sugar
1 Cup Flour
¼ Cup Butter

Whip eggs and sugar to a light foam. Sift flour and fold into egg mixture.

At the end, fold in melted butter and mix until incorporated.

Spread mixture into greased 8 inch cake pan approximately 1/8 inch thick and bake in oven at

375 degrees until golden brown (about 8 to 10 minutes)

Make 4 thin layers.

Let cool.

Pastry Cream

3 Cups Milk
¾ Cup Sugar
½ Cup Butter
½ Cup and 1 Tbs Cornstarch
3 Eggs
1 Cup Raspberry Jam

Stir 1 cup of milk into the cornstarch until dissolved

Add eggs to the same container and mix until everything is smooth liquid.

Bring rest of milk, sugar and butter to a boil.

While heat is on, add cornstarch and egg mixture and stir constantly until mix thickens.

Spread raspberry jam onto first layer of sponge cake.

Place second layer on top and repeat this procedure until all 4 layers are used.

Place this cake into 8 inch cake pan.

Once the pastry cream is cooked, pour it on top of the cake.

Let cool overnight. Slice into desired portions.

Rice Cream

YIELD: 10 servings

1lb Short-Grain White Rice (not instant)

1 tsp Salt

3 Cups Water

4 Cups Milk

2 Cups Heavy Cream

4 Tbs Sugar

2 tsp Vanilla Extract

Strawberry Sauce:

2 Cups Strawberry Preserves

1 Cup Water

1 Tbs Lemon Juice

Cook rice with water and salt for 15 minutes, covered

Add milk and cook for 30 minutes or until rice is tender and the mixture is thick

Chill rice in the refrigerator

Whip cream and sugar and vanilla

Gently fold whipped cream into chilled rice. Set aside in refrigerator

Place sauce ingredients in the work bowl of a blender. Mix until combined

Spoon rice mixture into serving cups

Garnish with strawberry sauce

White Chocolate Cappuccino Cheesecake

Pie Crust
1 Cup Oreo Crumbs
1 ½ Sticks of Butter
½ Cup Sugar
Mix all ingredients together.
Press into bottom of cake pan

Bottom Layer – Cappuccino Cheesecake
1 ½ Cup Heavy Cream
1 ½ Cup Cream Cheese
¾ Cup Sugar
1 ½ Tbs Gelatin
1/8 Cup Instant Coffee
¼ Cup Warm Water
Whip cream until firm and set aside
Cream sugar and cream cheese together until smooth
Fold heavy cream mixture into sugar and cream cheese mixture
Dissolve gelatin and coffee in water
In a microwave or double boiler, heat up this mixture to 180 digress
Do not bring to a boil! Fold the liquid into the mixture
Pour into cake pan and spread evenly
Put in the refrigerator for at least 2 hours

Top Layer – White Chocolate Filling

4oz of White Chocolate (*do not use chips*)
1 ½ Cup Heavy Cream

Melt white chocolate over double boiler
Whip up heavy cream to very soft peaks
Take ½ cup of this whipped cream and mix in the melted white
chocolate until smooth
Slowly add the rest of the whipped cream to the chocolate mixture.
Mixture should stay smooth
Place mixture of top of cappuccino filling and spread evenly
Let sit overnight in the refrigerator
Take out of the cake pan by inserting cake pan in hot water.
Slice into desired pieces

Kringle

3 Cups Flour
2 Tbs Malt
1/4 Cup Sugar
1 Tbs Yeast
6 Tbs Raisins
3 Cups Water
¼t Cardamom

Place all dry ingredients into mixing bowl using dough hook.
Mix for one minute on low speed.
Add water and mix on medium speed until dough forms.
At the very end, just before dough is done, add raisins.
Remove dough from bowl and scale into four ounce pieces.
Roll long strands and form into pretzels.
Let rise until doubled in size, then bake at 400° F. until golden
brown.

Icing

½ Cup Powdered Sugar
2tsp Evaporated Milk
¼tsp Vanilla Extract
Sliced Almonds
Mix powdered sugar, milk and vanilla extract together.
You can add a little more milk if too thick.
Pour icing in a plate.
Pour almonds in a plate.
Dip pretzel into icing and then into the almonds

Ring Cake

3 Cups Butter (*softened*)
1 ½ Cups Almond Paste
3 Cups Powdered Sugar
3tsp Almond Extract
6 Egg Yolks
7 ½ Cups Flour

In a large mixing bowl, cream butter, almond paste, powdered sugar,
and almond extract.

Beat in egg yolks.

Gradually add flour and mix until smooth.

Refrigerate until well chilled.

Place dough in a cookie press and press into ring molds,
which can be purchased at specialty stores.

If you don't want to invest in molds, shape the dough on
foil-covered cardboard into
26 rings graduating in size.

Start with a one inch ring and make each ring 1/2 inch larger than
the one before.

Bake at 350° F. for 15 minutes.

Frosting

1 ½ Cups Powdered Sugar
1 Egg White
1 tsp Lemon Juice
Stir all ingredients together.
Add additional powdered sugar if the frosting is not stiff enough.
Place in a pastry tube with a small round tip.
Drizzle some frosting on a platter (this will anchor cake).
Place the largest ring on the frosting.
Apply frosting in scallops on the first ring and place the next largest
ring on top of the first.
Continue until you have used all 26 rings.
The frosting will hold the rings in place.
Decorate with small Norwegian flags.

Chocolate Mousse Cake

Yield: 14 servings

1/2 – 10″ Chocolate Sponge Cake
2Tbs Rock Candy Syrup
1/8oz Triple Sec
3 1/2 Cups Heavy Cream
14oz Chocolate (*melted*)
6oz Chocolate Ganache (*for top, recipe below*)
4oz Chocolate Shavings
7oz Heavy Cream (*for rosettes*)
14 Chocolate Flowers (*for garnish*)

Ganache

8oz Semi-Sweet Chocolate
16oz Heavy Cream
10" round cake ring
10" cardboard circle
Melt chocolate in a hot water bath.
Melt ganache separately in a hot water bath.
Whip heavy cream until soft peaks are formed.
Do not overmix.
Refrigerate.
Cut sponge cake in half through the thickness.
Place cake on top of cardboard, cut side up.
Evenly sprinkle rock candy syrup over cake.
Place the metal cake ring around cake so that it is centered.
Fold melted chocolate into whipped cream.
Do not overmix.
Place chocolate mousse mixture on next and spread evenly over
entire cake.
The mousse must be smooth when finished.
Chill cake until the mousse has solidified.
Pour melted ganache over cake.
Make a smooth, even layer with a spatula.
Before serving, pipe a whipped cream rosette near the outer edge of
each slice.
Garnish with chocolate flowers that are leaning against the rosette.
Cut with a hot knife, cleaning knife after each cut.

School Bread

4 Cups Water
6 Tbs Yeast
7 Tbs Sugar
5 T Butter (*melted*)
1 tsp Cardamom
4 Cups Flour
1 Egg
1 Cup Coconut (*shredded*)
1 1/2 Cups Vanilla Custard
Heat water and butter to 95 degrees
Mix flour, sugar, cardamom, yeast, and egg together for five minutes until dough is stiff.
Form it like a ball and place in a bowl, cover with plastic wrap and let proof for 45 minutes, or until dough has doubled in size.
Roll the dough out like a sausage and cut into five ounce pieces.
Roll each piece into a ball and put them on a non-stick sheet pan and
let them proof for 30 minutes.
Bake for 15 minutes in 375 degree oven. Let cool.
Mix powdered sugar and water (use small amounts until proper consistency is achieved)
To make icing and place in shallow pan
Form hole in bread using finger.
Dip bread in icing (hole side down) and sprinkle with shredded coconut.
Using pastry bag, squeeze vanilla custard inside of hole and swirl at top for decoration.

Vanilla Custard

1 2/3 Cups Milk
1/4 Cup Sugar
1/4tsp Vanilla Extract
4 Egg Yolks
1 Tbs Cornstarch

In heavy saucepan bring milk to a boil. Set aside.

In bowl, beat eggs, sugar, and vanilla until the mixture doubles by volume.

Add the hot milk a few drops at a time to temper the eggs.
Mix well after each addition.

Place in metal mixing bowl and place over double boiler.

Dissolve cornstarch in a little water and add in a thin stream while stirring constantly until it thickens to proper consistency. It must not boil.

Cool by placing pan in ice bath.

The China Pavilion

The Epcot China Pavilion has some of the most interesting exhibits in the park. There are beautiful recreations of treasures and structures all over China. Some of the most interesting are easy to miss if you just breeze through.

When you walk into the pavilion, you will notice how serene everything is. The garden effect is very calming. Relax and enjoy walking through the chaos of a Chinese garden.

The big colorful centerpiece is a half-sized replica of The Temple of Heaven. The acoustics inside the dome are amazing.

The Food

There are two restaurants in the pavilion: One sit down and a fast food version outside. Nine Dragons is a sit down restaurant serving mass quantities of Chinese food. Lotus Blossom Cafe is a fast food restaurant with both indoor and outdoor seating.

Ginger Zinger

1 part Domaine de Canton ginger liqueur
1 part light rum
3 parts ginger ale
Stir and garnish with a lemon twist.

South Sea Breeze

1 part coconut rum
1 part pineapple juice
1 part orange juice
Stir and finish with a drizzle of grenadine to create the "sunset".

Shanghai Fusion

2 parts light rum
1 part cherry brandy
1 part plum wine
2 parts grapefruit juice
4 parts pineapple juice
Stir and serve.

Jade Beauty

1 part vodka
1 part Midori liqueur
2 parts pineapple juice
1 part Sprite
Gently stir and serve.

Heavenly Clouds

1 part coconut rum
1 part Midori liqueur
3 parts pineapple juice
Stir and then gently pour half & half on top (called a "float") and create the clouds. If you have trouble getting the cream to float, try pouring over the back of a spoon.

Spicy Beef in Sichuan Broth

Complete Dish:
10 ounces sliced beef
10 peppercorns
8 dried Sichuan pepper
2 ounces Shanghai bokchoy, blanched
1 tablespoon chopped garlic
1 tablespoon chopped scallion
2 tablespoon cooking oil
1 tablespoon Chinese cooking wine
1 cup water or chicken broth
3 to 4 tablespoon soy sauce, to taste
Beef Marinade
white pepper to taste
salt to taste
1 tablespoon corn starch
1 tablespoon water

Slice beef. Add in marinade. Put aside.

2. Heat 2 tablespoons of cooking oil in a frying pan over medium high heat. Stir in peppercorn. Stir fry peppercorn for about a minute or until fragrant.

Discard peppercorn.

Keep fragrant oil in frying pan. Stir in dried Sichuan pepper. Stir fry dried peppers until brown in color. Remove and put aside dried pepper.

With oil still in the frying pan, stir in chopped garlic and chili paste. Stir fry until fragrant. Add cooking wine, then water. Cook broth to a boil. Add soy sauce and a dash of white pepper. Quickly stir in sliced beef. Once beef is cooked, add blanched Shanghai bokchoy. Dish up. Top cooked beef and broth mixture with browned Sichuan pepper.

Serve immediately with steamed rice.

Saucy Chicken

Yield: 2 servings

3/4 pound chicken breasts, boneless

1 egg

1 teaspoon cornstarch

2 tablespoons peanut oil

3 onions, green

1 tablespoon peanut oil

1 tablespoon ginger, chopped

2 garlic cloves, crushed

1 tablespoon sherry

3 tablespoons soy sauce

1/2 tablespoon sugar

1/4 cup chicken stock

1/2 tablespoon white vinegar

1 1/2 tablespoons water

1 cup peanuts

Deep fry peanuts until golden and crunchy. Cut chicken meat into cubes. Toss with egg and cornstarch; add salt and white pepper to taste. Set aside to marinate for 30 minutes.

Add oil to wok and tilt pan to distribute.

When the temperature reaches 350, add chicken and stir fry Until 80% tender. Drain.

Cut green onions into 1/2 inch pieces. Dry wok; add green onions, oil, ginger, and garlic.

Stir fry for 1 minute

Then add chicken and stir together.

Add sherry, soy sauce, sugar, chicken broth, white vinegar, and cornstarch dissolved in water.

Stir in fried peanuts and stir fry until chicken is fully cooked.

Serve immediately with rice.

Pork Loin with XO Sauce

Yield: 4 servings

1 pound boneless pork loin, cut into thick slices
3 tablespoons vegetable oil
1 whole green onion, diced, for garnish
steamed rice for serving

Marinade

1 1/2 teaspoons salt
1 1/2 teaspoons dried chicken base
1 tablespoon each: Asian cooking wine, cornstarch and flour
1 egg
1 tablespoon sesame oil
white pepper to taste

XO Sauce

3 tablespoons cornstarch
1 1/2 teaspoons chicken bouillon
3 teaspoons soy sauce
1 1/2 teaspoons oyster sauce
2 tablespoons XO Paste (*seasoning paste sold in Asian grocery stores*)
2 tablespoons oil
1 tablespoon chopped garlic
2 tablespoons Asian cooking wine
1 tablespoon chicken bouillon
1 tablespoon sugar
white pepper to taste
1 tablespoon sesame oil
2/3 cup of water to thin sauce, if needed

Mix all marinade ingredients together.
Clean and pat the pork loin dry. Cut pork into 1/2 inch thick slices.
Marinate the pork in the refrigerator for at least 30 minutes.
Make XO Sauce and keep warm.
Heat vegetable oil in a frying pan. Sauté pork slices about 5 to 7
inches until golden brown.
Plate pork slices in a stack on a serving plate.
Pour XO sauce over pork slices. Garnish with green onions.
Serve with steamed rice and stir-fried green beans.

XO Sauce

In a small bowl, dissolve 3 tablespoons cornstarch in the chicken broth. Set aside.

In another small bowl, mix soy sauce, oyster sauce and XO paste. Set aside.

Heat the vegetable oil in saucepan.

Add garlic and sauté until golden.

Stir in XO sauce from above, then cooking wine.

Gradually stir in chicken bouillon, sugar, pepper to taste and sesame oil.

Dissolve 3 tablespoons cornstarch in 1/4 cup chicken broth.

Once mixture begins to bubble, stir in cornstarch mixture to thicken.

(You may need to add water it being like a thick sauce texture - not a gravy texture).

Strain, set aside, and keep warm.

Honey Sesame Chicken

Yield: 4 servings

10 to 12 ounces chicken breasts, cut into cubes

Marinade

1 teaspoon chicken base
(*not bouillon; base is a paste like mixture available in gourmet or larger supermarkets*)
Dash of white pepper
salt to taste
sugar to taste
1/2 teaspoon cooking wine
1/2 teaspoon sesame oil

Garnishes

toasted white sesame seeds
chopped green onions

Batter

3/4 cup all-purpose flour
1/4 cup cornstarch
1 heaping teaspoon baking powder
1/2 of a beaten egg
2 tablespoons oil
2/3 cup water
pinch of salt

Honey Sauce

1/8 cup, plus 1 tablespoon honey
1/4 cup sugar
1/8 cup ketchup
1 tablespoon white vinegar
Combine marinade ingredients and let cubed chicken soak in liquid
for 30 minutes.
Combine batter ingredients. Set aside.
Combine sauce ingredients. Set aside.
Heat cooking oil for frying, about 320 degrees
Using tongs, dip marinated chicken into batter and deep fry.
Heat honey sauce in a large wok. Turn off heat.
Add chicken pieces and toss to coat. Place chicken in green onions
and sesame seeds.

Kang Boa Chicken

Yield: 2 servings

3/4 pound chicken breasts, boneless
1 egg
1 teaspoon cornstarch
2 tablespoons peanut oil
3 onions, green
1 tablespoon peanut oil
1 tablespoon ginger, chopped
2 garlic cloves, crushed
1 tablespoon sherry
3 tablespoons soy sauce
1/2 tablespoon sugar
1/4 cup stock, chicken
1/2 tablespoon vinegar, white
1 1/2 tablespoon water
1 cup peanuts

Deep fry peanuts until golden and crunchy
Cut chicken meat into cubes.
Toss with egg and cornstarch; add salt and white pepper to taste.
Set aside to marinate for 30 minutes.
Add oil to wok and tilt pan to distribute.
When temperature reaches 350, add chicken and stir fry until 80% tender.
Drain.
Cut green onions into 1/2" pieces.
Dry wok, add green onions, oil, ginger, and garlic.
Stir fry for 1 minute, then add chicken and stir together.
Add sherry, soy sauce, sugar, chicken broth, white vinegar, and cornstarch dissolved in water.
Stir in fried peanuts and stir fry until chicken is fully cooked.

Serve immediately with rice.

Green Tea Ice Cream

2/3 cup water
4 green tea bags
1/2 cup sugar
1 cup half and half
1 cup heavy whipping cream

In a medium pot, heat the water to boiling.

Add the green tea bags, remove the pot from heat and let it steep for 5 to 7 minutes.

Remove the tea bags, squeezing them against the side of the pot with a spoon to get the entire liquid out.

Simmer over medium low heat for 10 to 15 minutes, or until the liquid is reduced by half.

Remove from heat and add the half and half and the sugar.

Let the mixture chill for a least 1 hour in the refrigerator.

Beat the whipping cream until soft peaks form and then fold in the green tea mixture.

Freeze in an ice cream maker, following manufacturer's directions.

Green Tea Frozen Yogurt

Serves 4

2 cups whole milk or low fat yogurt

2 teaspoons of green tea powder (*can add more for stronger taste*)

1/2 cup of sugar

In a blender, add milk, green tea powder and sugar. (*can you more powder for a stronger taste*)

Mix the ingredients well for three to five minutes until well blended.

Transfer the ingredients to the bowl of an ice cream maker and follow your manufacturer's directions.

If you do not have an ice maker, place into a freezer safe bowl cover it well.

Put the green tea yogurt mixture into the freezer for a few hours.

After the mixture is frozen, remove the bowl from the freezer and whisk again with a hand-help whisk until smooth and creamy.

Put it back in the freezer bowl and leave it in the freezers until frozen.

Take it out of the freezer and serve in small bowls.

Diao Yu Tai Cucumber Salad

2 Kirby cucumbers, about 4 to 5 inches long
1/4 teaspoon salt
1 tablespoon vegetable oil
4 dried red Sichuan peppers
1 cup of white vinegar
1 cup of sugar
Thoroughly wash unpeeled cucumbers and slice into 1/2 inch
pieces.
Toss cucumbers with salt in a colander.
Place colander over bowl and let stand 20 minutes.
Drain cucumbers and pat dry with paper towels.
Heat oil in wok over medium low heat
Add peppers and stir fry until pepper darkens to deeper red, 3 to 4
minutes.
Add vinegar and sugar; bring to a simmer, stirring until sugar
dissolves.
Remove from heat and cool to room temperature.
Pour mixture over drained cucumbers in a medium glass bowl
Cover and refrigerate for at least 24 hours.

Canton Beef

Yield: 4 servings

Beef

8 ounce beef flank steak
1 green pepper
1 red pepper
1 small onion
1 cup cooking oil

Marinade

4 tablespoons water
1/4 teaspoon salt
1/4 teaspoon chicken base
1/4 teaspoon sugar
1 egg white
1 teaspoon cornstarch
1/4 teaspoon sesame oil

Slice beef flank steak. Combine marinade ingredients.
Marinate beef in a bowl for at least 30 minutes.
Cut peppers and onion into bite-size pieces. Set aside.
Mix the sauce ingredients in a bowl and set aside.
Place about 1 cup of cooking oil in a heated wok or fry pan and heat
oil to medium heat.
Place marinated beef in heated oil and cook until almost done.
Drain beef into a strainer. Set aside. Leave about a teaspoon of oil in
the wok.
Place it back on the stove. Stir fry onion and peppers for 30 seconds.
Pour sauce mixture over onions and green peppers.
Stir occasionally with a spatula.
When sauce mixture begins to darken in color, place beef back into
the wok and stir fry swiftly.
The dish is done when the peppers have softened. Serve hot with
steamed white rice.

General Tso's Chicken

10-12 ounces thin-cut chicken, cut into strips and/or chunks
oil for frying

Marinade

1 teaspoon chicken base
1/2 teaspoon white pepper (*or more or less to taste*)
1 teaspoon sugar (*or more or less to taste*)
1/2 teaspoon cooking wine
1/2 teaspoon sesame oil

Batter

3/4 cup all-purpose flour
1/4 cup cornstarch
1 heaping teaspoon baking powder
1 egg, beaten
2 tablespoons oil
1 cup water
salt, to taste

Sauce

1 tablespoon soy sauce
2 teaspoons ketchup
5 tablespoons rice vinegar
5 tablespoons sugar
1/8 tablespoon black pepper
1/8 tablespoon chicken base
1 tablespoon corn starch
1 tablespoon vegetable oil

Combine all marinade ingredients and soak cubed chicken in marinade for at least 30 minutes or overnight.

Meanwhile, combine all batter ingredients, stir very well (*but do not beat*) and set aside.

If mixture is too thick (*it should be slightly thicker than waffle batter*), add as little water as needed to thin it out.

Set aside batter mixture.

Combine all sauce ingredients, mixing until completely blended and cornstarch is absorbed.

Set aside.

Pour cooking oil into a deep fryer or a large pot and heat to about 320 degrees.

Dip the marinated chicken a few pieces at a time into the batter, making sure that no pieces are stuck together and all parts of the chicken are completely covered in batter.

Drop carefully into oil and fry until golden and chicken is cooked (*cooking time varies depending on size of chicken... Test a piece for doneness to approximate cooking time if needed*)

Drain on paper towels. Keep warm. Take care that the oil doesn't get too hot; cooking the outside before the chicken is done, or too cold, causing the batter to become oily.

After all chicken is fried, heat sauce until it boils, darkens, and thickens slightly.
Quickly add chicken and toss to coat.
Serve immediately.

The Germany Pavilion

The Epcot Germany Pavilion is full of hand crafted goodies. The only thing German missing from this area is a Mercedes.

There are no rides located in the Germany Pavilion, only shops and a restaurant.

Between the Germany Pavilion and the Italy Pavilion is a small almost unforgotten area where Disney has set up a big miniature train set.

The Food

Come celebrate Octoberfest year round in the Biergarten. Sample traditional German foods like Spaetzle, Sauerbraten, Wiener schnitzel at a large buffet.

Wurstsalat

Yield: 6 servings

2 pounds (4 cups) assorted smoked German sausages

1 cup julienne red onion

1 cup German sweet pickles, cut on bias

1/2 cup German sweet mustard

1/2 cup German hot mustard

1 cup canola oil

1/2 cup balsamic vinegar

1/2 cup red wine vinegar

1/3 cup granulated sugar

Cut the assorted sausages on bias. Add the red onion and sweet pickles to the sausages.

Mix the mustards, oil, vinegars and sugar. Mix the dressing with sausages. Let set for 1 hour.

Schnitzel with Tomato and Mushroom Sauce

Schnitzel

4 (3 oz.) portions of veal, chicken, or pork cutlets
salt and black pepper to taste
2 eggs
1/2 cup bread crumbs

Sauce

4 ounces demi-glaze (*dry package classic sauce mix, look for brands such as Knorr*)
1 cup diced onion
1/2 cup large diced plum tomatoes
1 tsp. minced garlic
2 fresh rosemary sprigs
4 cups water
1 cup sliced mushrooms
1/2 cup small diced plum tomatoes
salt and pepper to taste
1 tablespoon freshly chopped parsley

Pound desired meat cutlet to tenderize. Rub in salt and pepper. Beat egg and dip each cutlet in the egg then the bread crumbs. Sauté until golden brown. Keep warm.

For the sauce, prepare the demi-glaze as directed on the package. Set aside. In a saucepan, saute the onion. Add large diced tomatoes, garlic, and rosemary and continue to saute until the onions are golden brown. Pour water to another saucepan and add the prepared demi-glaze sauce mix. Bring to a boil, stirring constantly. Reduce the heat and simmer 3 to 5 minutes, stirring occasionally until it thickens.

Add the sautéed vegetable mixture to the demi-glaze and let simmer 8 to 10 minutes. Strain. Sauté the mushrooms in a skillet. Add small diced tomatoes and cook until there is a little liquid left in the skillet. Season with salt and black pepper. Add the chopped parsley. Mix with the demi-glaze sauce.

To serve, place prepared cutlet on plate and spoon tomato and mushroom sauce over cutlet.

Sauerbraten

Marinade

1 pound onions, peeled, diced
1/2 pound carrots
1/2 pounds celery, diced
1 ounce minced garlic
1 quart red wine vinegar
1 quart red wine, 3 liter bottles
1/2 ounce fresh thyme
3 each whole cloves
1 each bay leaves
1 teaspoon salt
2 teaspoons cracked black pepper
10 pounds beef eye round

Combine all of the ingredients except the beef. Mix thoroughly. Add the beef eye round, and let marinade for at least 4 to 5 days.

Sauerbraten Sauce

6 ounces ginger snap cookies
1/4 cup tomato paste
8 ounces burgundy wine
64 ounces sauerbraten drippings
64 ounces demi-glaze
16 ounces sauerbraten marinade
8 ounces roux

Heat sauerbraten drippings, sauerbraten marinade, and demi-glaze to a simmer. Add the tomato paste.
Let simmer for about 30 minutes. Mix together the ginger snap cookies and burgundy wine in a separate container. Add this to the demi-glace mixture. Let simmer for another 30 minutes. If the sauce is too thin add enough roux to thicken. Strain sauce.
Sauerbraten Cooking Method: Braise the marinated eye rounds of beef. Sauté until all sides have been browned. Place in a roasting pan. Place half sauerbraten marinade and half demi-glace in the pan to cover 3/4 of the browned eye rounds of beef. Cover with foil.
Place in a 375 degree oven.
The sauerbraten can be removed from the oven when the meat is tender by the feel of a meat fork. About 3 to 4 hours.
NOTE: Reserve the liquid that the eye rounds were cooked. This will be used for the sauerbraten sauce. Also the sauerbraten is best when the marinated eye rounds are cooked the day before. Slice the cooked sauerbraten, and place in a pan. Ladle the sauerbraten sauce over the cooked sauerbraten and reheat in a 350 degree oven for about 30 to 45 minutes.

Raspberry Florentine Cookies

Serves: 8 people

Cookies

1 sheet (24 x 16 x ½ inches) Cookie Dough (*recipe below*)
2 cups raspberry jam
1 1/2 cup almond slices, blanched

Lay short cookie dough on sheet tray. Smear with jam (*apricot, raspberry, or jam of your choice*). Sprinkle with almonds. Bake at 375 degrees for 15 to 18 minutes. When cooled, cut into pieces.

Cookie Dough

2 cups all-purpose flour
1/2 teaspoon table salt
1/2 teaspoon baking powder
1 cup unsalted butter, softened
1 cup sugar
1 large egg
1.2 teaspoons vanilla

Whisk together in a bowl and set aside; flour, baking powder, salt.
Beat together butter and sugar in a large bowl with an electric mixer
at medium-high speed until pale and fluffy, about 3 minutes in a
standing mixer (*preferably fitted with paddle attachment*) or 6 with a
handheld. Beat in egg and vanilla. Reduce speed to low, then add
flour mixture and mix until just combined.
Place the dough on a paper lined sheet pan and press the dough out
as flat as possible so it can cool quickly. Cover in plastic wrap
refrigerate from 30 minutes to 4 hours, so it is firm.
Roll out the dough into a rectangle about 1/8 inches thick. Lay the
cookie dough on sheet tray. Smear with jam (*apricot, raspberry, or
jam of your choice*). Sprinkle with almonds. Bake at 375 degrees for
15 to 18 minutes. When cooled, cut into pieces.

Pork Shank Au Gratin

Yield: 6 servings

Main Dish

6 pork shanks
1 gallon vegetable stock
1 pound mashed potatoes
2 pounds sauerkraut

Onion Rings

1 medium onion. sliced
1 cup flour
1 cup vegetable shortening
2 cups milk
salt and pepper to taste
1 tablespoon freshly chopped chives

Cook the pork shanks in the vegetable stock until meat falls off the bone easily and skin is tender. This will take about 3 hours. When the shanks are ready take them out and let them cool. Reserve the cooking liquid/stock.

While the shanks are cooling prepare sauerkraut using some of the cooking liquid. Prepare mashed potatoes making sure they're nice and creamy. Pull the meat off the shanks and chop into bite size pieces. In an oven proof dish layer the bottom with sauerkraut and shank meat mix. Pipe or spoon mashed potatoes on top of this and finish it in the oven. Temperature should be set to about 450 degrees to allow the potatoes to develop nice golden color.

While this is cooking prepare onion rings which we will use to top off this nice dish. Slice onions into 1/6th of an inch rings and soak them in milk for 5 minutes. Next dredge them in the flour, salt and pepper mix, then fry to the light golden color in the heated shortening. Once ready rest the rings on the clean paper napkin. Carefully pull the oven proof dish out and top it off with onion rings and garnish with fresh chopped chives.

Roasted Pork, Potato Dumplings and Red Cabbage

Potato Dumplings

3 pounds peeled potatoes
1 1/4 cups all-purpose flour
2 eggs
1 teaspoon salt
1/4 teaspoon ground nutmeg
2 tablespoons butter
1/2 cup white bread crumbs

Cook the potatoes in water until tender. Cover and refrigerate 4 to 6 hours, then mash thoroughly. In a bowl, combine remaining ingredients with the mashed potatoes and mix well. Mixture should form a firm but light paste. Scoop out mixture to desired size and roll into a ball. Cook in simmering salted water for about 15 minutes. Remove with slotted spoon and drain well. Serve hot with roasted meat and gravy.

Nudel Gratin

Serves 8 to 10
2 cups heavy cream
2 eggs
1/4 teaspoon salt
pinch ground white pepper
pinch nutmeg
4 ounces Swiss cheese, shredded
4 ounces white cheddar cheese, shredded
1 pound cooked elbow macaroni

Preheat oven to 375 degrees. Spray a 16 by 9 inch baking dish with nonstick spray.
Combine cream, eggs, salt, pepper, and nutmeg in a large bowl, whisking to combine. Toss cheeses together in a small bowl until combined; remove 1 cup cheese and set aside. Stir remaining cheeses into cream mixture.
Cook macaroni until just tender; drain and add cream mixture, stirring immediately. Pour mixture into prepared baking dish. Cover with foil. Bake 30 minutes. Remove foil, and sprinkle reserved cheese over top of noodles. Bake 15 minutes longer. Cool 10 minutes before cutting into squares. Serve warm.

Macaroni Salad

Yield: 8 servings

2 cups elbow macaroni, dry
1/2 cup celery, diced
1/4 cup peas
1/2 cup diced tomato
1/4 cup onion
1 cup mayonnaise
1/2 cup pickle juice
1/4 cup white vinegar
1/4 cup sugar

Cook macaroni according to directions. Drain and cool macaroni. Mix all the ingredients in a bowl and add to the macaroni. Toss it well and adjust seasoning if necessary.

Linzer Torte

Serves: 8 people

1/2 cup soft butter
1/2 cup granulated sugar
2 cups ground hazelnuts
3 eggs
1 1/2 teaspoon cinnamon
1 cup all-purpose flour
1/2 teaspoon baking powder
1 cup raspberry jam filling

Mix flour, baking powder, hazelnuts and cinnamon together. Cream butter and sugar. Alternate, adding 1/2 cup of flour mixture at a time, adding 1 egg at a time while mixing. Grease 8 inch pan and spread half of the cake mixture on the bottom of the pan. Spread raspberry jam on top of the cake mixture. With the remainder of the mixture, use a pastry bag and pipe lattice design across the pan. Bake at 325 degrees for about 40 minutes, or until firm to touch. Let the cake stand for 10 minutes, then carefully flip cake out of the pan. Cool overnight.

Lentil Salad

1 pound lentils
1 cup small diced carrots
1 cup small diced celery
1 cup small diced onion
1 cup red wine vinegar
1 cup vegetable oil
1 tablespoon fresh chopped basil
1/2 tablespoon fresh minced garlic
1 tablespoon ham base
to taste salt
to taste black pepper

Place lentils in a saucepan with water to cover the lentils. Add the ham base. Bring to a boil, then reduce to a simmer until the lentils are soft but firm to taste. Drain the liquid from the cooked lentils and chill.

Meanwhile mix together the red wine vinegar, vegetable oil, basil, and garlic, salt, and black pepper. Then add the carrots, celery, and onions to the cooked lentils. Incorporate the dressing to the lentil mixture, and adjust seasoning.

Goulash Soup

Serves: 12 people

2 pounds beef stew meat
1 cup carrots, small dice
1 cup celery, small dice
2 cups onions, small dice
2 tablespoons garlic, minced
1/2 teaspoon cumin powder
2 tablespoons paprika
1/2 cup vegetable oil
1/2 cup flour
2 bay leaves
1 teaspoon Worcestershire sauce
3/4 cup burgundy wine
1 cup tomato paste
1 cup tomatoes, diced
5 bouillon cubes
2 quarts water
salt, to taste
black pepper, to taste

In a pot add the vegetable oil and beef. Sauté until browned. Then add the diced carrots, celery, onion, and garlic. Cook until the vegetables are soft but firm. Add the flour, cumin powder, paprika, and tomato paste and on a low flame and let cook for about 15 to 20 minutes, stirring occasionally to prevent from sticking to the pot. Then add the burgundy wine, Worcestershire sauce, diced tomatoes, bay leaves, water and bouillon cubes. Bring to a boil, then reduce the flame to a simmer until the beef is tender. Adjust seasonings with salt and black pepper.

Frikadelle

Yield: 4 servings

1 pound pork or beef-fresh ground

1/4 ounce minced garlic

3 1/8 ounce liquid eggs

1/2 ounce bread crumbs

5 ounces diced onion

To taste salt

To taste pepper

Mix all ingredients together. Form into ball and flatten. Grill until done.

Cracked Wheat Rye Bread

Yield: 2 loaves

2 cups cold milk

2 tablespoon sugar

4 tablespoons vegetable oil

2 tablespoons salt

3 eggs

2 cups coarse rye meal

5 1/2 cups bread flour

2 packages active dry yeast

Combine all ingredients in a large mixing bowl with an electric mixer equipped with a dough hook. Blend well for about 10 minutes. Remove dough hook and allow dough to rest for 20 minutes.

Turn dough out onto a floured board and knead lightly into a long roll.

Cut into 30 equal pieces and form into balls. Flatten slightly and place on a large, lightly greased baking sheet. Cover and let rise in a warm place until doubled in bulk. Bake in a preheated 400 degree oven for 20 minutes, or until lightly browned. Serve warm.

Bienenstich

Cake:

1 cup all-purpose flour

1 cup bread flour

1/4 cup granulated sugar

1/4 teaspoon salt

1 tablespoon yeast

2 tablespoon butter

2 each eggs

6 to 8 tablespoon milk

Topping:

1/4 cup sugar

3 tablespoons milk

1 cup almonds

Cake Method: Sift together the flours, salt and sugar. Add the eggs one at a time until incorporated. Then add the butter until mixed into flour mixture. Heat milk until it is warm to touch. Add yeast to milk and dissolve. In a mixing bowl, add the warm milk and yeast mixture to the flour until the dough pulls away from the sides but sticks to the bottom of the bowl. Place on a floured surface and roll into a 10 inch circle to the thickness of 1/4 inch. Then place in a greased 10-inch cake pan. Let sit in a warm place covered until the dough doubles in size.

Then place topping mixture on top of proofed cake and bake in a 350 degrees for 20 to 25 minutes or until the top is golden brown. Let cool on wire racks. Once cooled, slice in half lengthwise using a serrated knife. Brush both sides with the honey and sugar mixture. Then line a 10 inch cake pan with plastic wrap so it over hangs on the sides. Place the bottom of cake in the pan. Spread the pudding and whipped cream mixture on the bottom of the cake. Then place the top portion of the cake on the pudding mixture. Place in the refrigerator until cake sets. Remove from pan carefully from by pulling the plastic wrap. Serve.

Topping Method: Warm milk. Add the sugar and mix until well dissolved. Remove from heat and cool. Mix in the almonds. This will be used as a topping for the cake.

Filling

3 each instant vanilla pudding mix (3 1/8 ounce box)

4 cups milk

1 1/2 cups heavy cream

Add the pudding mix to the 4 cups of milk in a bowl. Beat with a wire whisk or electric mixer at low speed for 2 minutes. In a separate bowl whip the heavy cream until it forms soft peaks. Fold the heavy cream into the pudding mixture until well incorporated.

Honey and Sugar Mixture:

1/2 cup granulated sugar

1 cup water

1/4 cup honey

Mix together the ingredients. Heat until sugar dissolves. Cool at room temperature.

Rote Grütze

1/2 pound sour cherries, pitted (*can use canned*)
1/2 pound red currents
1/2 pound raspberries
1/2 pound strawberries, sliced
1/2 pound granulated sugar
8 ounces water
1/4 ounce gelatin powder
1 ounce corn starch

Clean and prepare all fruit, removing stems. In a large saucepan simmer red currents and sugar and half the water until slightly thickened. Then dissolve the gelatin in 2 ounces of the water. Place on the stove and heat until the gelatin dissolves. Then add the cornstarch to the remaining water and dissolve to make a smooth liquid.

Slowly pour the dissolved gelatin, the cornstarch and 1/2 of the remaining fruit into the red current mixture stirring constantly. Reduce heat and simmer for about one minute. Portion into glasses and chill for at least one hour. The consistency should not be as firm as jello or as runny as custard, but just that perfect point between. Serve with Vanilla Sauce or cream.

Potato Leek Soup

Serves: 8 people

3 cups potatoes, peeled and diced

1 cup onions, peeled and diced

1 cup leeks, cleaned and diced

5 cups chicken stock

1 cup heavy cream

2 teaspoons butter

salt, to taste

white ground pepper, to taste

1/4 cup chives, chopped for garnish

Saute the onions and leeks with the butter in a medium size pot. Then add the diced potatoes and cover with chicken stock. Cook until the potatoes are soft. Use hand blender and blend the soup until smooth, being careful as it will be hot. Stir in the heavy cream. Taste and season with salt and pepper. Just before serving garnish with the chopped chives and sauteed sliced leeks.

Black Forest Cake

Cake

5 eggs

1/4 teaspoon baking powder

3 egg yolks

1/4 teaspoon baking soda

2/3 cup sugar

1 1/2 teaspoons pure vanilla extract

3/4 cup cake flour, sifted

6 tablespoons cocoa, unsweetened (use a Dutch brand if possible, e.g. Droste)

Preheat oven to 350 degrees. Grease 3 (8-inch) round cake pans and line bottoms with waxed paper. In a medium sized mixing bowl, combine eggs, egg yolks, and sugar. Beat until thick and light. Sift together flour, cocoa, baking powder, and baking soda. Gradually fold flour mixture into egg mixture. Add vanilla extract last and pour batter into 3 cake pans. Bake for 18 to 20 minutes, or until tops spring back when pressed lightly with your finger. Cool on wire rack for 10 minutes before removing from pan.

Syrup

1/3 cup water
3 tablespoons kirsch (*cherry liqueur*)
1/2 cup sugar

Combine water and sugar in a small saucepan and bring it to a boil.
Remove mixture immediately and let cool. Stir in kirsch.

Filling & Frosting

1 1/4 cups cherry pie filling
2 1/2 cups heavy whipping cream, whipped
3 tablespoons kirsch
340 g dark chocolate, shaved

Mix together cherry pie filling and kirsch. Put 1 layer of cake on a flat plate. Brush top of first layer with syrup. Spread a layer of cherry mixture over syrup, spreading evenly. Add second layer of cake and spread with more syrup. Add another layer of cherry mixture, then a layer of whipped cream on top of that. Top with third layer of cake and brush with any remaining syrup. Frost top of cake with a thick layer of whipped cream, leaving sides exposed to show layers, and decorate with additional cherries. Sprinkle entire cake with shaved chocolate and refrigerate for 1 hour.

Bavarian Cheesecake

Cheesecake

6 ounces cream cheese
6 ounces baker's cheese
2 egg yolks
4 ounces granulated sugar
8 ounces sour cream
1 ounce lemon juice
12 ounces heavy cream
1/2 ounce gelatin
2 ounces water
Vanilla Sponge Cake (*recipe follows*)

Vanilla Sponge Cake

3/4 cup granulated sugar
4 egg yolks
1 teaspoon vanilla extract
3/4 cup all-purpose flour
3/4 teaspoon baking powder
1/2 teaspoon salt
4 egg whites

Preheat an oven to 375 degrees. Sift together the flour, baking powder, and salt.

In a mixer, add the egg yolks and sugar beat until light and creamy. Add the vanilla extract. Gradually add the flour mixture to the egg mixture. Beat until smooth. Whip the egg whites until stiff, but not dry. Gently fold this into the cake batter. Place into two separate greased and lined 8-inch round cake pans. Bake about 10 to 12 minutes.

Assembling Cake: Whip heavy cream until soft peaks. Set aside. Mix together in a mixing bowl the cream cheese, baker's cheese, egg yolks, and granulated sugar until smooth. Then add the sour cream and mix until smooth. Gently add the whipped mixture to the cheese mixture being careful not to over whip.

Dissolve the gelatin in the water over a double boiler until the mixture is clear. Be careful not to whip the gelatin so it does not get air bubbles in it. Add the gelatin mixture into the cheese mixture and fold quickly. When adding the gelatin mixture to the cheese mixture set the mixer on medium speed, and add it from the edge of the bowl, being careful not to get the gelatin on the whip or the side of the bowl so as to prevent lumping.

Using a springform pan, place one of the vanilla sponge cakes smooth side down. Immediately pour the cheese mixture on the cake, and smooth out surface. Then place the other cake on top with the smooth side out. Let set overnight. Remove the cake from the spring form pan. Sprinkle the top of the cake with powdered sugar. This cake can be served with any of your favorite fresh fruit sauce(s).

Cheddar Cheese Soup with Beer and Diced Onions

Yield: 3 gallons
1 pound butter
2.5 pounds onions, diced
1 pound all-purpose flour
4 ounces chicken base
2 gallons water
3 pounds shredded white cheddar cheese
1 (12 oz). bottle Octoberfest Beer
1 pinch white ground pepper
3 dashes Tabasco sauce

Saute the onions with the butter in kettle. Sweat until translucent.
Add flour, make a roux, cook for 4 min until flour starts to turn
blonde. Then add chicken stock and whisk vigorously. Cook until
the roux is cooked out, about 10 minutes. Add cheese slowly and
blend with a hand blender until smooth.

Season with pepper and tabasco.

Reheating for service: Place the beer on the stove to reheat just to
break the chill. Do not Boil. Slowly whisk the warmed beer into the
pot of soup and whisk vigorously to combine. Garnish with chives
and serve with pretzel croutons.

Soft Pretzels

1 package active dry yeast
1 1/2 cups warm water (*105 - 115 degrees*)
1 teaspoon salt
1 teaspoon sugar
4 cups all-purpose flour
2 eggs
2 tablespoons water
coarse salt
prepared mustard (*optional*)

Stir and dissolve yeast in warm water in a large mixing bowl. Stir in salt, sugar, and 2 cups of the flour. Beat until smooth. Stir in enough of the remaining flour to make dough easy to handle. Turn dough onto a lightly floured surface. Knead until smooth and elastic, about 5 minutes.

Cut dough into 3-ounce pieces and roll into a ball. Allow to rest for about 10 minutes. Roll out dough into strings and then twist dough pieces in the middle. Pick up dough string with two hands, each hand holding one end. Attach the ends to the dough in a pretzel shape. Place pretzel on baking sheet and allow to proof until pretzel string thickness is about double as thick (*place in a warm spot with a damp towel on top*).

Whisk the eggs with water. Brush egg wash on top of pretzels after they proof. Sprinkle with coarse salt. Put on to baking sheets and bake at 400 degrees for 10 to 12 minutes, until golden brown. Dip in prepared mustard if desired.

German Potato Salad

1/3 cup olive oil
2 teaspoons mixed herbs (tarragon, parsley & sorrel)
1/2 cup beef broth
1 tablespoon wine vinegar
1 tablespoon Dijon mustard
2 teaspoons sugar
3 teaspoons grated onion
4 large baking potatoes
salt & pepper

In a small bowl, combine olive oil, herbs, beef broth, vinegar, mustard, sugar & onion. Set aside. Steam potatoes until tender. Peel and slice potatoes into 1/8 inch slices while still warm. Add to oil mixture and mix carefully. Let stand one hour. Mix again without breaking potatoes and season to taste with salt & pepper. Refrigerate until ready to serve.

Apple Strudel with Vanilla Sauce
Strudel Dough

1 cup all-purpose flour
3/8 cup bread flour
1/2 teaspoon salt
1 egg yolk
1/2 teaspoon vegetable oil

Apple Strudel

prepared strudel dough, rested
1 stick butter, melted
1/2 cup toasted bread crumbs
1 1/2 pound apples, peeled, cored, and sliced thin
1/4 cup raisins
1/2 cup cinnamon sugar

Vanilla Sauce

2 egg yolks
1/3 cup granulated sugar
1 cup whole milk
1 cup heavy cream

For the Apple Strudel: Preheat the oven to 400 degrees. Stretch the dough until paper thin on a lint free tablecloth. Using a Pastry brush, cover two thirds of dough with melted butter. Once the dough is stretched out, sprinkle the toasted bread crumbs, about 3 inches wide, on the long end of the dough closet to you.

Place the sliced apples on the toasted bread crumbs. Sprinkle the raisins and cinnamon sugar on top of the apples. Grabbing a light free cloth on the side where the apple mixture is, roll the dough to the other en making sure that the apple mixture inside is even. Brush the outside of the dough with more of the melted butter. Bake for about 25 to 30 minutes or until the dough is golden brown. Let cool at room temperature for 10 to 15 minutes, then slice with a serrated knife into 4 equal portions. Spoon the Vanilla Sauce over the strudel.

To make the Vanilla Sauce: Combine the egg yolks and sugar in the bowl of a mixer. Beat with a wire attachment until thick an light. Scald the milk in a double boiler. Then heat the heavy cream in a separate saucepan, then add to the milk.

With the mixer running at low speed, very gradually pour the scalded milk into the milk mixture. Pour back into the double boiler. Heat it slowly, stirring constantly, until it thickened enough to coat the back of a spoon. Remove from the double boiler and set it in a pan of cold water. Stir in the vanilla. Stir the sauce occasionally as it cools.

Vegetable Quiche

Filling
1 zucchini cut into 1/4 inch cubes
1/4 medium onion cut in 1/4 inch cubes
1 medium tomato cut into 1/4 inch cubes
6-8 ounces shredded Swiss cheese
1 teaspoon thyme, minced
1 teaspoon rosemary, minced
Quiche Liquid
3 eggs
1 cup half & half
1 cup heavy cream
Whisk together.

Combine filling ingredients, season with salt & pepper; you want about a 50-50 mix of cheese and vegetables.

Place in a pie shell and cover with quiche liquid. Place in a preheated 300 degree oven and bake for 45 minutes to one hour until top is golden brown. Remove from oven allow to rest for 15 minutes before slicing.

Strawberry Tart

Dough

5 cups sifted flour

pinch of salt

1 1/4 cup sugar

9-14 tablespoons unsalted butter

3 eggs

1 tablespoon orange blossom water, or any other flavored water

Tart

strawberries, cleaned and hulled - 5 per tart

almond cream - 2 ounces per tart

apricot glaze - 1 ounce per tart

Napoleon

1 pound puff pastry
2 cups pastry cream
3/4 cup Chantilly Cream (*recipe below*)
confectioner's sugar
Vanilla Pastry Cream
2 cups milk
1/2 vanilla bean, split in half lengthwise
6 egg yolks
2/3 cup granulated sugar
4 teaspoons flour or corn starch

Chocolate Mousse

Makes 3 cups

5 ounces semi-sweet chocolate
2 egg yolks, lightly beaten
1/4 cup heavy cream
1 teaspoon pure vanilla extract
3 egg whites
1/4 cup sugar

Melt chocolate in a double-boiler over warm water.
Remove from heat. Combine egg yolks and cream and gradually
add chocolate, stirring rapidly.
Add vanilla. Beat egg whites with sugar until stiff peaks form.
Gently fold egg whites into chocolate mixture.
Spoon mousse into a decorative mold or individual serving glasses
and chill until firm, about 2 hours.

The Italy Pavilion

The Epcot Italy Pavilion is one of the most beautiful areas of the park. The statues, the architecture the fountains it's all beautiful. You can also get some good food and do some serious shopping.

All around the Italy pavilion there are beautiful things to see. Even the buildings create the look of Rome, Venice, and even Florence.

As you stroll through the pavilion, you'll see what looks like the Trevi Fountain, architecture taken from the Sistine Chapel. And a recreation of St. Mark's Campanile (bell tower), and a replica of the Doge's Palace.

Everywhere you look there is something beautiful to see. Even the new section with Via Napoli will remind you of the streets of Napoli.

The Food

Want some Italian food? You're in luck. This is the place to get some good Italian food and even a good pizza made from ingredients shipped over from the mother country.

Tutto Italia Ristorante is the restaurant that dominates this area. The restaurant is run by world famous California chef Joachim Splichal.

The other restaurant in Italy is Via Napoli. It's operated by the same company that runs Tutto Italia. Via Napoli specializes in Pizza. They offer an original pizza with ingredients that are shipped from Naples.

Campari & Soda

1 part Campari
2 parts seltzer
Stir and serve.

Aperol

Just Aperol over ice.

Aperol Sour

1 part Aperol
1 part sweet and sour mix

Negroni

1 part gin
1 part sweet vermouth
and 1 part Campari.

Red Passion

1 part Campari
2 parts grapefruit juice
1 part seltzer
Stir and serve.

Pomegranate Cosmopolitan

1 part Pama liqueur
1 part Citron Vodka
2 parts cranberry juice
squeeze of lime
Shake vigorously with ice and serve in a martini glass.

Roberto Cavalli Martini

Pour a small amount of dry vermouth into a chilled martini glass, tilt the glass so the vermouth coats the interior of the glass and pour out the rest. Shake the Roberto Cavalli Vodka with ice and strain into the prepared glass and garnish with a caper.

Carpano Punt E Mes

Dry vermouth over ice. Carpano is the original vermouth, invented in the late 1700's.

Frizzante

1 part campari
2 parts mandarin (or substitute orange) juice
2 parts Prosecco or other brut champagne

Bellini

1 part Monin or Island Oasis peach puree
4 parts champagne

Gnocchi with Spinach and Gorgonzola Cream Sauce

2 eggs
1/2 teaspoon salt
1/8 tablespoon ground black pepper
1/8 teaspoon ground nutmeg
1 (16 oz.) container ricotta cheese
1 (10 oz.) box frozen chopped spinach, thawed and squeezed dry
1 1/4 cups all-purpose flour
2 cups heavy cream
3 tablespoons dry white wine
1 teaspoon brandy extract
1 pinch ground nutmeg to taste
2 ounces crumbled Gorgonzola cheese
salt and pepper to taste

Beat eggs with salt, pepper, nutmeg in a large bowl.
Mix in ricotta cheese and spinach until evenly blended.
Continue mixing in the flour, 1/4 cup at a time until a soft dough forms.
If the dough is still sticky, add an additional 1/4 cup of flour.
Cover, and place into refrigerator.
Bring a large pot of lightly salted water to a boil over high heat.
Divide the gnocchi dough into 4 pieces, and roll into 1/2 inch thick ropes on a floured surface.
Slice each rope into 1/2 inch pieces.
Gently boil the gnocchi until they float in the water, 3 to 4 minutes.
Drain in a colander, and set aside.

Meanwhile, pour cream, wine, brandy extract, and 1 pinch of nutmeg into a saucepan.

Bring to a simmer, then remove from heat and whisk in the Gorgonzola cheese; season to taste with salt and pepper.

Toss the gnocchi with the Gorgonzola sauce, and serve immediately.

Lasagna al Forno

Yield: 10 portions

6 Fresh Pasta Sheets (precooked)
1/2 Cup Tutto Italia Pomodoro Ragout
2 Quarts Tutto Italia Béchamel Sauce
3 Quarts Tutto Italia Bolognese Sauce
4 Cups Grated Parmesan Cheese
1 Cup Shredded Mozzarella Cheese
2 Tablespoons Extra Virgin olive Oil

In a deep 13x9 pan, evenly spread around the olive oil, and then add the Pomodoro sauce, again evenly spreading across the bottom of the pan. Place you first pasta sheet , making sure to center it and firmly pressing it to the bottom of the pan. Place 2 cups of the Bolognese sauce in the pan and spread evenly across the pan using a spoon or rubber spatula, and sprinkle generously with the grated parmesan cheese. Place another pasta sheet on top of the Bolognese layer, again firmly pressing it down. Add 1 cup of Béchamel sauce to the pasta sheet and evenly spread it around. Sprinkle generously with the grated parmesan cheese. Repeat the process, continuing the alternating layers until all 6 layers are completed. On the final layer add the mozzarella cheese. Bake uncovered at 250 degrees for approximately 1 hour and 15 minutes, or until internal temperature has reach 165 degrees. Allow to rest for at least 10 to 15 minutes before cutting. Top with hot Pomodoro sauce and more grated parmesan cheese.

Fresh Pasta

7 Cups All-Purpose Flour
8 Each Whole Eggs
1 teaspoon Salt

In a kitchen aid mixer with the dough hook attachment, add the eggs and salt. Turn the machine on speed 2, and slowly add flour, just enough at a time that the eggs absorb the flour. Once all the flour has been added, and the dough has formed, remove from the machine. Form into a ball, and wrap in plastic wrap. Allow to rest for 30 minutes at room temperature. Cut into quarters, and press into flat discs, to feed into the pasta machine. Start at the highest number, and work you way down to number 3 for the lasagna. Pass the dough through that machine at least twice on each number. Cut into 13 inch long pieces, you should end up with roughly 10.
To Cook: In a 12 quart sauce pot, bring cold salted water to a gentle boil. Blanch the pasta sheets one at time, until they just begin to float. Rinse under cold water to stop the cooking process, and layer between wax paper until ready for use. Then can be refrigerated overnight after being cooked. Yield: 10 sheets.

Pomodoro Sauce

4 1 # Cans Imported Plum Tomatoes in Tomato Sauce
1 large Yellow Onion, diced
2 Cloves Garlic, chopped
1/2 Cup Extra Virgin Olive Oil
2 Tablespoons Kosher Salt
2 teaspoons Ground White Pepper
6 Leaves Fresh Basil Leaves, chopped

Crush the tomatoes by hand in a large bowl, by squeezing them. Cook the onions in the olive oil until clear over medium heat in a heavy bottomed 12 quart sauce pan. Add the garlic and cook till just fragrant. Add the crushed tomatoes, salt, and pepper. Bring to a boil, and then lower heat to a simmer. Cook for at least 1 hour, stirring occasionally. Add basil leaves, and remove from heat. Yield: 2 quarts.

Béchamel Sauce

2 Quarts Milk
1 Stick Unsalted Butter
4 Ounces All-Purpose Flour
1 teaspoon Ground Nutmeg
1 teaspoon Ground White Pepper
2 Tablespoons Kosher Salt

In a heavy bottomed sauce pot, over medium heat, melt butter. Once the butter is fully melted, add the flour, mixing completely together. Cook the mixture for at least one minute, stirring constantly. Add the milk into the mixture using a whisk. Bring to a boil, and then lower heat to a simmer. Season with salt, pepper, and nutmeg. Cook for at least 1 hour, stirring occasionally. Yield: 2 quarts.

Bolognese Sauce

1 Each Yellow Onion, fine diced
3 Ribs Celery, fine diced
1 Each Carrots, fine diced
3 Cloves Garlic, chopped
1/2 Cup Extra Virgin Olive Oil
1 Tablespoon Dried Thyme Leaves
2 Each Bay Leaves
1 Pound Ground Beef
2 Cup Tutto Italia Pomodoro Sauce
1/2 Cup White Wine
1/2 Cup Heavy Cream
2 Tablespoons Kosher Salt
2 teaspoons Ground Black pepper

In a heavy bottomed sauce pot, over medium heat, cook carrots, onions, celery, and garlic till onions are clear and soft. Add the ground beef and cook all the way through, making sure to break it up as much as possible. Add the dried herbs, Pomodoro sauce, wine, cream, salt, and pepper. Bring to a boil, and then lower heat to a simmer. Cook for at least 1 hour, stirring occasionally.
Serve. Yield: 2 quarts

Casarecci with Sausage

16 ounces cavatelli pasta
20 ounces homemade marinara sauce or your favorite jar sauce if
you so choose
1 ounce grated Romano
1 ounce butter
1/3 ounce fresh basil leaves
sweet or mild Italian sausage bulk

Cook pasta until al dente in a pot of boiling, salted water. Heat the
marinara sauce in a large saucepan. Reserve about 1 1/2 cups of the
sauce. Set aside.

Cook the sausage over medium heat, stirring until sausage is broken
up and fully cooked. Add the cooked pasta, butter and sauce toss
well. Add cavatelli pasta.

Top with grated Romano cheese and garnish with fresh basil.

Carciofi Pizza

9 ounces fresh prepared pizza dough
3/4 cup shredded mozzarella cheese
3/4 cup shredded fontina cheese
7 ounces canned plain artichokes (*not marinated*), drained, rinsed,
and cut into quarters (*if not already*)
2 tablespoons white truffle oil
flour, for rolling out dough
olive oil

Lightly oil a plate, place dough on plate, and let sit out for at least
an hour.

Place dough on floured surface and roll to 13 inch diameter.

Preheat grill to 425 degrees.

Place dough on preheated grill and cook for 2 to 3 minutes, until
browned and grill marks appear, then turn over. Drizzle olive oil on
browned crust, add artichokes and cheese, and then close grill lid.

Cook 2 to 3 minutes more, just until cheese is melted.

Remove from grill and place on pizza peel or cookie sheet.

Drizzle with white truffle oil and serve.

Zeppole di Ricotta

1 1/4 cup flour
1/2 cup sugar
4 teaspoons baking powder
pinch salt
2 1/4 cups ricotta cheese
4 eggs
1 teaspoon vanilla extract
vegetable oil for frying
powdered sugar for dusting

Whisk together flour, sugar, baking powder, and salt in a large bowl.
Add ricotta, eggs and vanilla; stir well to combine.
Pour oil into a deep fryer or saucepan to several inches deep, and heat to 350.
Drop batter by heaping teaspoonful into hot oil, a few at a time.
Fry until golden brown, turning once, 3 to 4 minutes. Drain on paper towels.
Dust with powdered sugar and serve hot.

The American Adventure Pavilion

The American Adventure is the host pavilion for the World Showcase. It's located right in the middle. If you line up the entrance and Spaceship Earth (the big silver ball), it will point right at the pavilion.

Inside this massive Colonial structure is a restaurant, a museum and a very large attraction. The restaurant serves hot dogs and hamburgers (standard American fast food). The museum has a huge rotunda and several exhibits that are historic and interesting. The attraction is very patriotic and has the biggest, most technologically advanced stage every built.

Outside, there are historic shows. The Fife and Drum Corp performs on select days. There are flag ceremonies during the day.

The Food

The American Adventure Pavilion does not offer the exotic cuisines found at the other countries. But what they do offer is some great American favorites like BBQ ribs, clam chowder and cheesecake. And of course good old American apple pie!

BBQ Ribs

(serves 4 people)
12 oz smoked baby back ribs
2 oz BBQ sauce
1 each mini corn muffin

BBQ sauce

1 cup BBQ sauce
1/4 cup apple juice
1 tbsp. apple cider vinegar
2 tbsp. maple syrup
1/4 tsp black pepper

Mix together the apple juice, apple cider vinegar, and maple syrup.
Add to the BBQ sauce and then season with the black pepper.
If the consistency of the sauce is too thick, add enough apple juice
until you have the desired thickness.

New England Clam Chowder

(Yields 3 qts. / 10 servings)

1 qt. canned, minced clams with juice or fresh shucked clams w/
juice
3/4 qt. water
5 oz. salt pork, ground or cut into fine dice
1/2 lbs. onions, small dice
White pepper
2 oz. flour
1 lbs. potatoes, small dice
2 1/2 qts Milk, hot
1 cup heavy cream, hot
salt

Drain the clams. If you are using fresh clams, chop them, being sure
to save all the juice
Combine the juice and water in a saucepan. Bring to a boil.
Remove from heat and keep the liquid hot.
In a heavy sauce pot or stock pot, render the salt pork over medium
heat
Add the onions and cook slowly until they are soft, but do not
brown.
Add the flour and stir to make a roux.
Cook the roux slowly for 3-4 minutes, but do not let it brown.
Using a wire whip, slowly stir the clam liquid and water into the
roux. Bring to a boil, string constantly to make sure the liquid is
smooth.

Add the potatoes. Simmer until tender (If you are using large, tough
"chowder" clams, pass them once through a grinder and add them
with the potatoes).

Stir in the clams and the hot milk and cream. Heat gently but do
not boil.

Season to taste with salt and white pepper.

Bake at 400 degrees (F) for 40 minutes

Creamy Clam Chowder
& Garlic Thyme Crackers

Serves 4-6

Garlic Thyme Crackers

2 cups Oyster Crackers
1/4 cup Butter
1 Tbsp. Garlic Powder
1/4 tsp. Dried Thyme
1 cup Onions, diced

Clam Chowder

3 ea. 6 oz. Cans Chopped Clams
3 cups Clam Juice, bottled
1 cup Celery, diced
2 cups Potatoes, diced & par-boiled
3/4 cup Unsalted Butter
3/4 cup All Purpose Flour
1/2 tsp. Salt
1/8 tsp. White Pepper, ground
1 pint Heavy Cream
1/2 cup Garlic Thyme Crackers

Preparation for Crackers

Pre-heat oven to 200 degrees.
Melt butter with garlic powder and thyme. Spread crackers on cookie sheet. Drizzle butter mixture over top cracker to lightly coat. Toss crackers. Place in oven and bake for 7-12 minutes or until crackers are golden brown.
Remove from oven and let sit for 10 minutes. Serve crackers with clam chowder.
May be stored in an airtight container and kept for 4 days.

Preparation for Clam Chowder

Add clam juice to a small pot. Drain clams in can and reserve liquid. Heat juice to a simmer.

Add juice from canned clams. In a medium pot melt butter. Add onions and sauté until translucent. Add flour and whisk into onions and butter.

Cook for 2-3 minutes. Slowly whisk in heated clam juice, making sure there are no lumps.

Bring to a boil, and then reduce heat to a simmer.

Add celery and potatoes. Bring back to a simmer. Cook for 10 minutes, stirring often. Add clams and heat through. Whisk in cream. Heat to a simmer and serve.

Garnish with garlic and thyme crackers.

Crab Cakes with Broccoli and Slaw & Blood Peach Sauce

Serves 4-6

Crab Cakes

1 lb. Lump Crab Meat
3 Tbs. Celery, minced
2 Tbs. Onion, minced
1 Tbs. Scallion, sliced thin
2 Tbs. Lemon Juice
3 Tbs. Dijon Mustard
1 tsp. Worcestershire Sauce
2 Tbs. Parsley, chopped
1 1/2 cup Mayonnaise
Old Bay Seasoning
1/8 tsp. Black Pepper
1/2 cup Japanese Breadcrumbs

Broccoli Slaw

1 bag Broccoli Slaw
2 cups Coleslaw Dressing (Store bought or homemade)
Homemade coleslaw dressing:
1 cup Mayonnaise or Miracle Whip
1 tsp Lemon juice
3/4 cup sugar
1/4 cup whole milk
Mix all ingredients together and stir until mixture is smooth.

Blood Peach Mayonnaise

8 ea. Blood Peaches
1/4 cup Mayonnaise
1/2 tsp. Lemon Juice
1/8 tsp. Salt
1/8 tsp. Cayenne Pepper

Preparation for Crab Cakes

In a medium bowl add onions, celery, scallions and parsley. Mix
well.
Add crabmeat (shells removed) and mix lightly.
Add lemon juice, Worcestershire sauce and mustard. Mix together.
Add 1 cup mayonnaise and breadcrumbs. Mix.
Add Old Bay seasoning and pepper to taste.
If mixture is too dry add the other 1/2 cup of mayonnaise.
Heat a medium sauté pan over medium heat.
Add a small amount of oil to prevent sticking.
Shape crabmeat into patties and cook until golden brown.
Turn crab cakes over and continue until heated through. Serve with
broccoli slaw and peach sauce.

Preparation for Broccoli Slaw

Add slaw mix and dressing into medium bowl and mix.
Keep refrigerated until ready to serve.

Preparation for Blood Peach Mayonnaise

Cut peaches (may use other types of peaches) and remove pit. Peel
off skin. Add peaches to blender and process until pureed.
Add peach puree to a small bowl.
Add mayonnaise and lemon juice. Mix well.
Season with salt and cayenne pepper.
Keep refrigerated until needed.

Cheesecake

Serves 4-6

Graham Cracker Crust

2 cups graham cracker crumbs
1/4 cup corn syrup
1/4 cup melted butter

Cheesecake

1 cup powder sugar
1 pound cream cheese
1/4 cup sour cream
3 eggs
1/2 teaspoon vanilla

Preheat oven to 300ºF degrees.

Prepare crust by blending together crumbs, corn syrup and butter. Press into cake pan sprayed with vegetable spray.

Prepare cheesecake filling by mixing together powder sugar, cream cheese, sour cream and vanilla until smooth.

Add one egg at a time and keep mixing until mixture is completely smooth. (Do not mix on high speed, as you will incorporate too much air into mixture, which would create air bubbles that would result in uneven surface after baking).

Pour cheese mixture on top of crumbs and flatten with spatula.

Place cake pan into sheet pan filled with water and bake for approximately 90 minutes.

Check internal temperature of cheesecake with a thermometer probe.

If temperature is 170ºF, the cheesecake is done.

Remove cheesecake from oven. Cool overnight.

Next day, tip cheesecake out of pan and slice.

Serve with fruit sauce or fresh berries.

Apple Pie

(Serves 6 people)

Pie Crust

8 oz pastry flour
6 oz shortening
2.5 oz cold water
Rub shortening into flour to form nuggets the size of walnuts.
Add water and mix quickly until dough forms.

Filling

1 lb apples

4 oz water

3 oz sugar

1 oz cornstarch

1/2 oz butter

Pinch of cinnamon

Juice of 1/2 lemon

Dissolve cornstarch in 1.5 oz of the water.

Bring the rest of the water, cinnamon, butter and sugar to a boil.

Add cornstarch mixture and stir constantly until mixture thickens.

Add the apples and mix well.

Roll out pie crust and lay out 9 inch pie tin. Add the filling.

Roll out second half of crust and cover pie.

Bake at 400 degrees (F) for 40 minutes

The Japan Pavilion

The Japan Pavilion is the one of those pavilions in the World Showcase that doesn't have a ride or a movie or a show. It wasn't supposed to be that way, but that's the way it worked out. It's easy to think you could just walk by without slowing down. Most visitors don't plan to stop in this area, but they should, because there's some good stuff here.

Just like the nation it represents, you'll find order and tranquility all around. It can get very crowded just like much of Japan. You'll find the hustle and bustle of a Tokyo street and the serenity that can only be found in a Japanese garden.

The Food

The Japan Pavilion is home to some great restaurants. If you don't stop here for any other reason, check out one of the great dining options.

Teppan Edo is Japan's signature restaurant. Teppan Edo replaced Teppanyaki in 2007. Teppanyaki is a form of cooking where food is cooked on a hot grill. At Teppan Edo you sit around a grill and a chef prepares your meal. The chef puts on a show as he or she cooks. It's not only great food, but also an interesting show.

Tokyo Dining is not just eating in the biggest city in Japan, it's also an eating area outside of Teppan Edo. Tokyo Dining is a combination sushi bar and full service restaurant. At Tokyo Dining you can get everything from Octopus sushi (and all other kinds of sushi) to a New York Strip steak and much more.

The menu at Tokyo dining includes sushi, sashimi, tempura and grilled steaks and chicken. The seating is in an open area. There are several tables mainly for 2 or 4 guests.

Katsura Grill is the third dining area in the Epcot Japan pavilion. It's tucked away on the other side of the pavilion from Tokyo Dining and Teppan Edo. Katsura Grill (formerly Yakitori House) serves traditional Japanese noodle dishes and Teriyake and Tempura.

Matsu

½oz Gin
1oz Melon Liqueur
2oz Pineapple Juice
1oz Lemon Bar Mix
4oz Crushed Ice
Straw
Mix all ingredients in a blender until frothy.
Serve in a tall glass with a straw.

Asian Slaw and Vinaigrette

1 Cup Edible-Pod Pea Slivers
1 Cup Carrots (*shredded*)
2 Cups Cabbage (*finely shredded*)
½ Cup Fresh Ginger (*fine slivers*)
1½ Sesame Oil
¼ Cup Reduced-Sodium Soy Sauce
1½ Tbsp. Rice Wine Vinegar
1½ Tbsp. Mirin (*sweet sake*)
1½ Tbsp. Sugar
1½ Tbsp. Lime Juice
1 Clove Garlic (*minced*)

In a bowl, mix peas, carrots and cabbage.
In a 6-8″ frying pan on medium-high heat, mix ginger and sesame oil;
stir until golden, 2-3 minutes.
Remove from heat and stir in soy sauce, rice vinegar, mirin, sugar, lime juice, and garlic.

Ginger Dressing

Yield: 2 Quarts

2oz Ginger Root

1 medium Onion (*cut in quarters*)

3 Cups Vegetable Oil

1 Cup Vinegar

1 3/4 Cups Soy Sauce

1 1/2 Tbsp. Tomato Paste

1/4 Lemon (*juiced*)

1 Clove Garlic

1 3/4 Cups Water

Soak ginger root in cold water for a few minutes to make it easier to remove outer peel.

Peel and cut into quarters.

Combine all ingredients in a food processor with a steel blade and blend until smooth.

Refrigerate.

Ginger Sauce

Yield: 10 servings
6oz Onion
1oz Ginger Root
6Tbsp. Soy Sauce
3/4 Cup Water
Pinch of Parsley Flakes
1/2 of a Lemon
2 Tbsp. Rice Vinegar

Place onion, ginger root, soy sauce, water, parsley flakes, lemon and rice vinegar in blender.
Blend (puree) all ingredients at high speed until well blended.
Serve with seafood or beef

Mustard Sauce

Yield: 10 servings
1oz Onion
1 Tbsp. Mustard (*dry powder*)
1 Tbsp. Sesame Seeds (*roasted*)
1/2 Cup Soy Sauce
2 Tbsp. Vegetable Oil
3/4 Cup Water
2 Tbsp. Heavy Cream

Place onion, mustard, sesame seeds, soy sauce, vegetable oil and water in blender.

Blend (puree) all ingredients at high speed until well blended.

Add heavy cream just before serving (stir into sauce, do not use blender).

Japanese Curry with Beef

8oz Beef (for stew, cut into 3/4″ chunks)
8oz Onion
6oz Carrot
6oz Potato
8oz S&B Curry Mix
2tsp. Butter
2tsp. Vegetable Oil
1 Tlbs. S&B curry powder
2tsp. Honey
Pinch of Pepper
Pinch of Salt
3¾ Cups Water
Short-Grain Rice

Add vegetable oil to large sauté pan over medium heat.
Add beef chunks, then salt & pepper to taste; brown.
Chop onion, carrot, & potato and add to sauté pan.
Sauté ingredients until vegetables are tender.
Add water and curry powder to pan; bring to a boil.
Reduce heat, skim off the surface, and then add curry mix cubes; stir until dissolved.
Add honey and butter to pan; continue to simmer over low heat until beef is tender,
Approximately 30 minutes.
Once beef is tender, remove from heat.
Serve hot over short-grain rice.

Sukiyaki

Yield: 4 serving servings
1lb Beef (*paper thin slice*)
1 large Onion
1 Bunch Green Onion
½lb Carrot
2 Packs Japanese Noodle

Dashi

1 Cup Water
1 inch square Konbu (*Sea Weed*)
1/2 Cup Bonito Flakes
Place in a saucepan with konbu and water and soak for 2 hours.
Bring saucepan to a rapid simmer over high heat.
Remove saucepan from heat, adding bonito flakes.
Let stand for 3 minutes, strain through into a bowl.

Sukiyaki Sauce

1/5 Cup Soy Sauce
1/5 Cup Mirin (*Sweet cooking Sake*)
1 Cup Dashi (*Fish Stock*)
Heat sukiyaki pot
1 tablespoon fat in pot, add beef slices and sear on both sides.
Add sauce, vegetables cook as desired.

Yakitori Sauce

1/4 Cup Sake Wine

1 Cup Mirin Wine

1 Cup Soy Sauce

1 Tbsp Sugar

2 Tbsp Cornstarch

1/3 Cup Water

Combine sake and mirin wine in a medium saucepan and bring to a boil.

Add soy sauce and sugar.

Let simmer covered, for 30 minutes.

Dissolve cornstarch in water and add to boiling mixture.

Cook and stir until mixture boils and is thickened.

Serve hot over baked, broiled or roasted chicken.

The Morocco Pavilion

The Morocco pavilion may be the least visited area in all of Disney World. Which is a shame really. There is some great history here, along with some beautiful workmanship. King Hassan II sent several top artists to assist with the design of the buildings and assisted in the mosaic work.

The pavilion is divided into two sections, the old city and the new city. There is a lot of traditional artwork, food and even belly dancers.

The Old City

The Medina or the old city is set up to be a busy marketplace. You will find baskets, jewelry, leather goods, brass pots and much more. The gate to the Medina is a replica of the Bab Boujouloud gate. The real gate actually sits in front of a fountain very much like the one in the courtyard.

The New City

The Ville Nouvelle or new city is towered over by the Koutoubia Minaret which is a replica of the famous one in Marrakesh. The new city is vibrant, full of color and amazing architecture. In the new city, you will find a modern art gallery.

The Food

There are two restaurants in this area. The full service restaurant is called Restaurant Marrakesh. The quick service restaurant is called Tangerine Cafe. You might not find much of a wait at these restaurants. They aren't very popular, but the reviews are usually very good. Both serve authentic Moroccan cuisine which isn't real popular with most American guests.

Moroccarita

2 parts vodka
1 part triple sec
1 part lemon juice
1 part lime juice
2 parts sweet and sour mix

Habibi Daiquiri

1 part rum
2 parts sweet and sour mix
1 part Monin or Island Oasis strawberry puree or frozen
strawberries in syrup
Blend with ice, pour into a glass and top with a small amount of
orange blossom water.

Sultan's Colada

2 parts rum
1 part almond liqueur
3 parts pineapple juice
1.5 parts crème de coconut such as Coco Lopez
Blend with ice and serve.

Marrakesh Express

1 part Cruzan coconut rum
2 parts orange juice
2 parts pineapple juice
Stir and then top with 1 part Myer's dark rum.

Casablanca Sunset

1 part apricot brandy
1 part peach schnapps
2 parts orange juice
2 parts cranberry juice
Stir and serve.

Tangier's Breeze

1 part peach vodka
1 part Midori
3 parts pineapple juice
Stir and serve.

Sahara Splash

1 part vodka
1 part Midori
2 parts cranberry juice
1 part seltzer
Stir and serve.

Tangerine Coffee

1 part Grand Marnier
3 parts good strong coffee
top with whipped cream

Kasbah Coffee

1 part Frangelico
3 parts good, strong coffee
top with whipped cream

Casablanca Coffee

1 part Stoli Vanil Vodka
3 parts good, strong coffee,
top with whipped cream

Harira Soup

1/2 pound uncooked meat (*lamb, beef or chicken*), chopped into 1/2 inch pieces

several soup bones (*optional*)

3 tablespoons vegetable oil

1 bunch cilantro (*coriander*), finely chopped to yield about 1/4 cup

1 bunch fresh parsley, finely chopped to yield about 1/4 cup

1 or 2 celery stalks with leaves, finely chopped

1 large onion, grated

1 handful of dried chickpeas, soaked and then peeled

1 teaspoon ground cinnamon

1 tablespoon ground ginger

1 1/2 teaspoons pepper

1 tablespoon kosher salt

1/2 teaspoon turmeric or 1/4 teaspoon yellow colorant

6 large tomatoes (*about 2 pounds*), peeled, seeded and pureed

3 cups water

2 to 3 tablespoons dried lentils, picked over and washed

3 tablespoons tomato paste, mixed evenly into 1 or 2 cups of water

2 to 3 tablespoons uncooked rice or uncooked broken vermicelli

1 cup flour mixed with 2 cups water

Ahead of Time

Make sure you have all the ingredients. Before you begin cooking the soup:

Pick the parsley and cilantro leaves from their stems. Small pieces of stem are all right, but discard long, thick pieces with no leaves. Wash the herbs, drain well, and finely chop them by hand or with a food processor.

Soak and skin the chickpeas. (*You might want to soak them the night before you cook.*)

Peel, seed and puree the tomatoes in a blender or food processor. Or, stew the tomatoes and pass them through a food mill to remove the seeds and skin. Pick through the lentils and wash them. Assemble the remaining ingredients and follow the steps below.

Brown the Meat

Put the meat, soup bones and oil into a 6-quart or larger pressure cooker. Over medium heat, cook the meat for a few minutes, stirring to brown all sides.

Make the Stock

Add the cilantro, parsley, celery, onion, chickpeas, spices and tomatoes. Stir in 3 cups of water.

Cover tightly, and heat over high heat until pressure is achieved. Reduce the heat to medium, and cook for 20 to 30 minutes. Remove from the heat and release the pressure.

Make the Soup

Add the lentils, tomato paste mixture, and 2 quarts of water to the stock. Set aside (*but don't add yet*) either the rice or vermicelli. Cover the pot and heat the soup over high heat until pressure is achieved. Reduce the heat to medium and continue cooking.

If adding rice: Cook the soup on pressure for 30 minutes. Release the pressure, and add the rice. Cover, and cook with pressure for an additional 15 minutes.

If adding vermicelli: Cook the soup on pressure for 45 minutes. Release the pressure, and add the vermicelli. Simmer the soup, uncovered, for 5 to 10 minutes or until the vermicelli is plump and cooked.

Thicken the Soup

While the soup is cooking, make a (*soup thickener*) by mixing together the 1 cup of flour with 2 cups of water. Set the mixture aside, and stir or whisk it occasionally. The flour will eventually blend with the water. If the mixture is not smooth when you're ready to use it, pass it through a sieve to remove lumps.

Once the rice (or vermicelli) has cooked, taste the soup for seasoning.

Add salt or pepper if desired.

Bring the soup to a full simmer. Slowly — and in a thin stream — pour in the flour mixture. Stir constantly and keep the soup simmering so the flour doesn't stick to the bottom. You will notice the soup beginning to thicken when you've used approximately half the flour mixture. The thickness of harira is up to you. Some like to thicken the broth so that it achieves a cream-like consistency.

Simmer the thickened soup, stirring occasionally, for 5 to 10 minutes to cook off the taste of the flour. Remove the soup from the heat.

Vegetable Couscous

Yield: 4 servings
1 pound carrots
1/2 pound turnips
1/2 pound cabbage
1/2 pound zucchini
1/2 pound tomatoes
1 1/2 ounces chick peas (garbanzo) precooked
1 ounce onion, chopped
1 small bunch parsley, chopped
1 small bunch cilantro, chopped
1 teaspoon ginger
4 tablespoons oil
1-2 drops yellow food coloring
pinch of saffron
1 teaspoon tomato paste
salt and pepper to taste
1 gallon water
1 (12 oz.) box of couscous

In a large pot bring the 1 gallon water to a boil; add chopped onion, oil, saffron, yellow food coloring, parsley, cilantro, tomato paste, and salt and pepper. Bring water back to a boil.

Then start adding vegetables as follow:

Add the carrots, boil 5 minutes.

Add the turnips, boil for 5 minutes.

Add the cabbage, boil for 5 minutes.

Add the zucchini and boil for 20 minutes, or as needed for vegetables to cook.

To cook couscous semolina, follow instructions on box.

To Serve: Place couscous semolina on plate and cover with vegetables and cooking liquid.

You can also add either chicken or lamb to this dish. If you are
adding chicken or lamb, put the chicken or lamb in the boiling
water with the onion, oil, saffron, yellow food coloring, parsley,
cilantro, tomato paste, salt and pepper and boil for one hour, then
add the vegetables and cook for another one half-hour, or as needed
for vegetables to cook.

Seafood Bastilla

Serves 4-6

1 pinch saffron
1 pound fish - cod, Mahi Mahi, grouper, etc.
1 pound (70-90) count peeled shrimp
1 onion chopped
1 tablespoon parsley, chopped
1 tablespoon coriander, chopped
1 cup mushrooms, sliced
1 tablespoon garlic chopped
1/2 cup olive oil
1 teaspoon salt
1 teaspoon white pepper
1/2 cup lemon juice

Saute fish, shrimp, and all other ingredients together until done. Drain, and put drained sauce back into the fry pan.

Add the following to sauce and cook:

1/2 cup crabmeat chopped
12 eggs scrambled
1 thinly grated zucchini
3 thinly grated carrots

Cook until done. Drain and then mix all your cooked ingredients together. Let mixture cool.

Place 2 ounces of cooled mixture on egg roll sheet and roll to desired size. Brush with melted butter. Bake until golden brown.

Moroccan Grilled Salmon

Serves 4
1 cup olive oil
1 tablespoon garlic, minced
1 teaspoon salt
1 teaspoon pepper
1 teaspoon cumin
1 tablespoon paprika
1 teaspoon fresh coriander, chopped
1/4 cup fresh lemon juice
4 (8 oz.) salmon fillets

Combine all ingredients except salmon in a large bowl or dish. Place salmon fillets in the mixture and marinate in the refrigerator for 2 to 6 hours.

To grill: Oil the grill and heat the coals to medium. Place the salmon skin side up on the grill and cook for 5 to 7 minutes on each side or until done. When the center flakes away easily, and the fish is an opaque pink.

Moroccan Vegetable Rice

Serves 6
2 cups long grain white rice
4 cups water
1/2 cup olive oil
1/2 cup frozen peas
1/2 cup frozen corn
1/2 cup grated carrots
1/2 cup tomato paste
2 teaspoons salt
1 tsp white pepper
pinch of saffron
Preheat the oven to 350 degrees.
Combine all ingredients in a 2 1/2 to 3 quart baking dish and
combine thoroughly with a whisk.
Cover the dish and bake for 1 hour until all the liquid is absorbed.
Stir the rice before serving.
(*If you are using a gourmet rice, such as basmati, the cooking time
will be a bit longer.*)

Roast Lamb Meshoui

4 servings

4 (14-16 oz.) lamb shanks

1 celery stalk, coarsely chopped

1 tomato, cut into quarters

1 carrot, sliced

1/2 onion, sliced

1 zucchini, sliced

1 green pepper, coarsely chopped

1 yam, coarsely chopped

1 can chickpeas drained

1/2 head cabbage, julienne

1/2 bunch parsley and 1/2 bunch cilantro tied together

1/2 tablespoon turmeric

salt and pepper to taste

1/2 tablespoon paprika

1/2 tablespoon cumin

1 pinch saffron

1/2 tablespoon ground ginger

1 teaspoon chopped garlic

1 teaspoon olive oil

1/2 stick butter

Place lamb shanks in a roasting pan.
Roast at 300 degrees for 30 minutes, or until meat is brown. Brown the onion in half the butter and olive oil and add to lamb. Then add the vegetables (except the carrots, yams, green peppers and zucchini), and then add the spices.

Add 2 cups water and roast until meat is tender. Add the carrot, yam and cook for 10 minutes, then add the green pepper and zucchini and cook until they are tender. Remove the meat, and reduce the sauce a little. Then strain the sauce and serve over the lamb.

Note: All other Meshoui recipes say to rub the lamb with salt, pepper, paprika, and chopped garlic before roasting. The lamb then gets put in the center of the roasting pan, and the vegetables go around it. They get roasted uncovered for about 30 minutes, and then covered with water and roasted until done (usually 1 1/2 hours for a leg of lamb.)

Meatball Kebobs

1 pound lean ground beef or lamb
3/4 cup chicken broth
1/2 cup plain dry
bread crumbs
1/2 cup finely
chopped onion
1/3 cup each chopped cilantro and parsley
1 tablespoon paprika
1 teaspoon each ground cumin, salt and pepper
Mix ingredients until very well blended. Form into 12 balls. Thread
3 on each of four (12 inch long skewers. Grill or broil 5 minutes per
side or until cooked through and a thermometer inserted in centers
registers 160 degrees.

Lentil Salad

Yield: 4 servings

12 ounces lentils

3 ounces mayonnaise

1 ounce chopped green bell pepper

1 ounce chopped red bell pepper

1 ounce chopped red onions

1 teaspoon lemon juice

salt

pepper

Boil the lentils (*do not overcook*),
wash, drain and let cool. Add all the ingredients and mix well.
Serve chilled.

Lemon Chicken

Serves 5 people
5 pieces of chicken
2 1/2 ounces ground ginger
2 1/2 ounces black pepper
4 ounces salt
1 ounce olive oil
3 1/2 ounces salted butter
pinch of saffron
2 1/2 ounces sweet butter
10 cinnamon sticks
1 ounce fresh chopped coriander (*Chinese parsley*)
5 cloves chopped frsh garlic
5 lemon pickles, quartered
1/2 pound green olives pitted
1/2 teaspoon yellow food coloring
1 1/2 pounds Spanish onions, chopped
1 pint water

Clean chicken and set aside. In small mixing bowl, combine ginger, pepper, salt, yellow food coloring and salted butter, mix well. Rub mixture on chicken.

In casserole dish place sweet butter and olive oil, coating sides and bottom equally, Add chicken, sprinkle evenly with onions, saffron, coriander and garlic. Place cinnamon sticks in corners and middle of casserole dish.

Add water, place on stove and bring to a boil. Put in 350 degree oven and cook for 45 minutes.

Arrange couscous in tagine (Moroccan serving dish with cover), place lemon chicken in the center and add vegetables on top of chicken.

Jasmina Salad

Serves 4
2 fresh medium tomatoes
1 medium cucumber
1/3 cup onion, finely chopped
1/4 bunch parsley, finely chopped
coriander, finely chopped
pinch ground cumin
salt and white pepper to taste
2 tablespoons fresh lemon juice
2 tablespoons salad oil
12 grilled boneless, skinless chicken breast (*chicken is optional*)
Mix all the ingredients except the tomatoes, cucumbers and chicken breasts. Cut and dice the tomatoes into small cubes. Peel and seed the cucumber, then dice into approximate size of tomato cubes. Place cubed tomatoes and cucumbers in a dish and spread the other mixed ingredients over them.
Refrigerate for 1 hour or more before serving.
To serve, place a leaf of lettuce on a plate and arrange a serving of the salad. Place 3 grilled chicken breasts on top of salad for each serving.
Marinade and seasoning for chicken breast:
Season to taste with olive oil, salt, pepper, and garlic.

Goat Cheese Appetizer

8 ounces goat cheese
1/2 cup Kalamata olives, pitted and chopped
1/2 cucumber, seeded, peeled and chopped
1 clove garlic chopped
1 tablespoon half and half
salt and pepper to taste

Mix all ingredients. Let it sit for 30 minutes to 1 hour.

Moroccan Salad Combo

Green Pepper & Tomatoes, Marinated Olives,
Carrots, Potatoes, and Cucumber Salad

Serves: 4
1 cucumber, peeled and diced
2 tomatoes, diced
2 tablespoons red onion, finely chopped
1 heaping teaspoon fresh parsley, finely chopped
1 heaping teaspoon fresh cilantro, finely chopped
2 tablespoons olive oil
2 tablespoons white vinegar
1 teaspoon cumin
pinch of white pepper
salt, to taste
2 cups mixed greens
Mix all ingredients except greens in a large bowl and combine well.
Season with salt to taste
Serve over the greens.

Couscous Salad

Yield:4 servings
olive oil
1/2 of a red onion
1 teaspoon chopped garlic
1/2 of a sweet red bell pepper
1/2 of a sweet green bell pepper
1/2 of a chopped zucchini
salt and freshly ground pepper to taste
nutmeg to taste
cinnamon to taste
1/2 cup olive oil
1/4 cup raisins
1/4 cup chickpeas (*garbanzo beans*)
1 cup orange juice
12 ounces cooked plain couscous
2 tablespoons chopped fresh parsley
1/2 cup tangerine segments or mandarin orange segments
mint sprig for garnish

In a large nonstick skillet, sauté onion, garlic, sweet bell peppers and zucchini in olive oil.

Season with salt, pepper, nutmeg and cinnamon.

Add 1/2 cup olive oil to vegetables along with raisins, chickpeas and orange juice.

Toss vegetable mixture with couscous and pan juices.

Add parsley and gently fold in citrus segments.

Mound mixture onto a serving platter and garnish with mint.

Couscous Mrouzia

2 onions sliced
1 cup dry raisins soaked in hot water
1 tablespoon ground ginger
1 tablespoon turmeric
1/2 cup sugar
1 tablespoon cinnamon
1 pinch saffron
1 cup honey
salt and black pepper to taste
In a small pot, sweat onions. Add all ingredients and cook for at least 45 minutes
Beef Tagine for Mrouzia:
1 pound stew beef cut into cubes
1/2 cup chopped tomatoes
1/2 cup chopped onions
1 tablespoon ginger
1 tablespoon black pepper
1 tablespoon turmeric
1 tablespoon salt
1 cup water
In a large pot, sauté all ingredients except water until brown. Add 1 cup of water and cook until tender. Both items are served on couscous.

Chicken Bastilla

Serves 12

3 whole chicken breasts (*about 1 pound each*)
1/2 pound butter
1 1/2 pounds finely chopped onions
1 teaspoon ginger
1 pinch saffron
1 quart water
2 cinnamon sticks
1 teaspoon cinnamon
salt and white pepper to taste

Cook chicken breasts with all above ingredients until tender.
Remove chicken and allow to drain. Return drained liquid to the
pan the chicken was cooked in. Set chicken aside to cool.

12 raw eggs - beaten well
13 Bastilla leaves

Scramble eggs with a hand whip until well mixed. Add eggs to the
liquid the chicken was cooked in. Allow to boil slowly, stirring
constantly. Turn down to simmer and stir only enough to keep eggs
from browning for about 10-15 minutes.
Do not cover. Drain in colander or strainer and reserve liquid.
Set aside and allow to cool.

1 1/2 cups finely chopped almonds
1/4 cup granulated sugar

Add granulated sugar to crushed almonds. Mix well.

Shred the chicken with your hands, and then mix with the egg mixture. Mix well. If it feels dry or crumbles, it needs some of the reserved liquid. Add just enough to moisten it. Mix well again.

Cut one Bastilla leaf into 12 pie-shaped pieces. Lay out one whole Bastilla leaf and then lay one of the 12 pie-shaped pieces in the center of it.

On the center piece, add 1 tablespoon of almond mixture, then on top of the almonds, add 3 ounces chicken mixture. Add another 1 tablespoon almond on top of the chicken mixture. Fold the Bastilla leaf around the mixture, bringing the sides to the top and pleating them.

Repeat this procedure for each of the appetizers.

1 cup Ten-X powdered sugar
cinnamon

Put Bastilla, pleated side down, on a greased cookie sheet. Using a pastry brush, lightly brush top of Bastilla with vegetable oil.

Cook in a 350-degree oven until golden brown.

Turn Bastilla over and brown other side. Remove from oven.

Let sit for 2-3 minutes.

Sprinkle powdered sugar from a sifter on top.

To design with cinnamon, pinch cinnamon between thumb and forefinger and release it in a sliding motion on top of Bastilla.

This takes practice.

Brochette of Chicken

24 oz. chicken breast, cut into 1 inch cubes
1/2 bunch fresh parsley, finely chopped
1/2 bunch coriander (or cilantro), fresh and finely chopped
1 teaspoon fresh garlic, minced
1/2 teaspoon cumin
salt and white pepper to taste
1/4 cup olive oil
2 drops yellow food coloring
1 tablespoon lemon juice
8 (8 inch) skewer sticks
Mix all ingredients well.
Put 4 ounces of chicken on each skewer stick.
Cook over a bed of hot coals on a barbecue grill or broil in oven
until tender, about 5 minutes.

Beef Shish Kebabs

24 ounces beef tenderloin, cut into 1 inch cubes
1/2 cup finely chopped onions
2 tablespoons finely chopped parsley
2 tablespoons finely chopped coriander
1 tablespoon paprika
1/4 cup olive oil
salt and white pepper to taste
1 teaspoon cumin
8 (8 inch) skewer sticks
Combine all ingredients and mix well.
Put 4 ounces of beef on each skewer stick.
Cook over a bed of hot coals or in the broiler for about 5 to 8
minutes.

The France Pavilion

The France Pavilion is home to the World Showcase's top French restaurant. It's also a great place to grab a quick bite, see some historic sites, and sit down and watch a good movie.

You will see the streets of Paris as they looked in "the beautiful time" or as the French say La Belle Epoque. You can even see a small version of the Eiffel Tower .

Keep your eyes peeled; you never know when Belle from Beauty and the Beast might be strolling around enjoying a beautiful day.

Food

France is the home of haute cuisine. The world looks at French food as the best available and uses it as a basis for a lot of menus at lots of restaurants around the world.

The top restaurant is Le Chefs de France. Some of the top French chefs in the world have contributed to the menu and even oversee the production of the food. The menu has lots of French sounding food.

A year or so ago, Disney added Remy from Ratatouille to the menu. No not to eat, but to visit with. Several times per day, Remy comes and visits tables spreading his little humor.

Bistro de Paris is a located above Le Chefs de France, on the second floor. This is an upscale restaurant that actually has a dress code. (The dress code prohibits swim suits, hats, tank tops, cut offs or torn clothing.) This restaurant has a very upscale dinner menu and is only open for dinner, including upscale pricing. Lobster, duck breast and rack of lamb are the stars of the show.

Boulangerie Pâtisserie is a pastry shop, hence the French word Pâtisserie, which means pastry, which serves tarts, cookies, eclairs, turnovers, and much, much more.

There is also a crepe wagon across from Bistro de Paris. Crepes are thin pancakes. These are stuffed with fillings like strawberries and showered with powdered sugar.

Cafes et Digestifs

1 part Grand Marnier
3 parts good coffee
top with whipped cream

Pernod-Ricard

3 parts Pernod

1 part water

Pour gently, DON'T stir and serve immediately.

Pernod turns from clear to a cloudy opaque when mixed with water.

Allow the guest to stir for the effect to happen in front of them.

Grand Marnier & Grey Goose Orange Slush

1 part Grand Marnier
1 part Grey Goose Vodka
2 parts sweet and sour mix
1 part simple syrup.
Blend with ice to create your frozen cocktail.
Sorry, you'll have to add orange food coloring if you want it orange,
just like they do at Epcot.

Grey Goose Citron Lemonade Slush

2 parts Grey Goose Citron (or other) citrus vodka
2 parts sweet and sour mix
1 part simple syrup
Blend with ice.

Seared Scallops with Tomato Coulis and Rice Galette

Yield: 4 servings.
3 shallots, finely chopped
chopped fresh tarragon
butter for sautéing
2 cups white wine
2 tablespoons vinegar
1 cup heavy cream
14 ounces unsalted butter
2 chopped tomatoes
salt and freshly ground pepper to taste
12 scallops
Rice Galette (*see note*)
sautéed pear baby tomatoes, fried herb leaves and fresh dill for garnish

Sauté shallots and tarragon in butter Add wine, vinegar.
Let cook for few minutes.
Add cream. Let cook until mixture reduces in volume by half. Add butter a little at a time.
Add tomatoes, stirring. Season with salt pepper.
Season scallops with salt, pepper.
Sauté in butter until golden and cooked.
Serve on top of rice Galette.
Ladle sauce around edges. Garnish.

Rice Galette

Sauté 1 chopped onion in butter.

Add 5 ounces risotto, chicken and clam bases and saffron to taste.

When risotto is cooked, mix in 2 ounces Parmesan and 4 ounces of butter.

Mixture should be thick. Place on sheet pan and flatten out.

Cool in the refrigerator.

Once cooled cut into squares or triangles.

Sauté in butter until browned for presentation

Note: flavoring bases are concentrated pastes sold in all major supermarkets. Look for them on the top shelves in the area where they sell bouillon. Never substitute bouillon!

Matignon

Yield: 4 servings

Cake

4 eggs
8 ounces sugar
8 ounces flour

Ganache

2 cups heavy cream
8 ounces dark chocolate
3 ounces butter
2 ounces sugar
1 vanilla bean
Syrup made from mixture of rum, sugar and Kahlua

Crème Anglaise

2 cups milk, scalded
5 tablespoons sugar
Pinch of salt
4 egg yolks, lightly beaten
1 teaspoon vanilla
ice water

Cake

Whip 4 eggs with 8 ounces of sugar over low heat until creamy.
Remove and slowly mix in 8 ounces of flour.
Spread cake mixture on a flat pan with 1/4 inch sides and bake in a
300 F oven for 10 minutes.

Ganache

Place cream, butter, sugar and vanilla bean in a pan.
Bring to a boil. Remove from heat.
Pour cream mixture over chocolate and whip together.

Crème Anglaise

Heat milk, sugar and salt in the top of double boiler over medium heat,
stirring until sugar dissolves.
Stir a little milk mixture into egg yolks, and then add eggs to milk mixture.
Set mixture in pan over barely simmering water.
Cook, stirring until thickened, 2 to 3 minutes.
Mix in vanilla. Cool mixture quickly by setting the pan in ice water and stirring briskly. Refrigerate until ready to use.
Assembly: Cut the cake the size of the 1 1/2-cup capacity domed molds.
Dampen the pieces with the syrup.
In the molds pour in the ganache to fill half.
On top of the ganache put a piece of the cake; cover with more of the ganache until it has filled the mold.
You should use about 1 1/2 cups of the ganache.
After the ganache has hardened, invert the molds onto a plate and serve with crème Anglaise.

Coq au Vin

Yield: 4 servings

2 pounds bone-in chicken parts (*breasts, wings, drumsticks, thighs*)
1/2 teaspoon each: coarse salt and freshly ground pepper
1 1/2 ounces salt-pork fat
2 tablespoons butter
6 pearl onions, peeled
1/4 pound whole mushrooms, washed and stems trimmed
2 tablespoons all-purpose flour
1 garlic clove, peeled and crushed
1 (750 ml) bottle Beaujolais wine
2 sprigs fresh thyme or 2 teaspoons dried
2 sprigs fresh parsley or 1 tablespoon dried
2 bay leaves
1 to 1 1/2 cups chicken stock
hot cooked noodles for serving

Season chicken with salt and pepper and set aside.
Cut pork fat into 1/2-inch cubes and place in small skillet.
Cover with cold water and bring to a simmer on medium heat,
then reduce heat and simmer for 5 minutes.
Drain and pat cubes dry with paper towels.
Heat oven to 350 degrees.
In large oven-proof pan, heat butter, pork fat and pearl onions on
medium-high heat. When onions are golden, remove them along
with pork fat with slotted spoon. In remaining butter, cook
mushrooms on high heat, about 2 minutes on each side, until lightly
browned.
Remove with slotted spoon and set aside.
In same pan, sauté chicken on high heat, about 2 minutes per side.
Sprinkle the chicken with flour and place, uncovered, in the oven
for five minutes. Remove chicken from oven and reduce heat to 250

degrees. Add garlic to chicken and stir 1 minute. Return pan to
stovetop. Add wine and bring to boil, stirring constantly. Add herbs,
onions, pork fat and mushrooms.
If necessary, add stock to cover meat.
Cover pan and bake in oven for 1 1/2 hours.
Remove pan from oven. Put chicken on shallow platter. Strain
remaining sauce to remove vegetables. Discard fresh herbs. Taste
sauce and adjust seasonings as desired with salt and pepper. Ladle
sauce and vegetables over and around chicken. Serve with hot
noodles.

Flatbread Appetizers

Dough for Tart
1/2 pound flour
3 1/2 ounces rendered pork fat
1 teaspoon yeast
1/2 cup tepid water
.7 ounces lard

Add the yeast to tepid water and stir. Mound the flour on a table; add a pinch of salt, the rendered pork fat and the lard, work in with your fingers. Add the yeast and water and knead. Form a ball, cover with a cloth and place in a warm place for 2 hours.

Work the dough out with the palm of your hand and roll to ¼ centimeter thick and a 9 inch circle.

Onion Tart

7 ounces crème fraîche
3 large onions, sliced very thin
7 ounces smoked bacon
chopped and precooked pepper
Pour the crème fraîche over the tart shell, layer with onions and
bacon, and pepper to taste.
Put in the oven and bake for 5 minutes at 400 degrees.

Mushroom Tart

In oil, place sliced mushrooms: shiitake, button & Portobello in pan and sauté until tender. Meanwhile mix together 3 cheeses, shredded: Parmesan, Gruyere, Emmental and Provolone. Place mushrooms on tart, cover with cheese and bake at 400 degrees for about 5 minutes.

Tomato Tart

2 large tomatoes, peeled and diced
1 bunch fresh basil, coarsely chopped
goat cheese, cut in pieces
Tomato Compote (*recipe below*)
pepper

On the dough, layer the compote, diced tomatoes and basil. Drizzle with olive oil and pepper to taste. Place the cheese pieces on top of the pizza and bake for 5 minutes in 400 degree oven.

Tomato Compote:

3 large tomatoes
3 cloves garlic
1 bunch fresh thyme leaves
1/4 cup olive oil
Blanch the tomatoes in a pot of boiling salted water for 15 to 20 seconds, just long enough so that you will be able to peel the skin. Drain the tomatoes, and peel their skins. Then chop with the garlic and thyme, until garlic and thyme are minced. Add the chopped tomatoes, garlic, olive oil and thyme to the saucepan.
Stir to combine, adjust heat to a simmer, and let reduce until thick.

Vegetable Lasagna

Yield: 4 servings

1 cup shredded Swiss cheese

2 red bell peppers cut in 1/2 inch cubes

2 green bell peppers cut in 1/2 inch cubes

1 pound eggplant cut in 1/2 inch cubes

1 pound zucchini cut in 1/2 inch cubes

1 1/2 cup tomato sauce

1 large onion cut in 1/2" cubes

5 pasta sheets

1 sprig thyme

1 sprig rosemary

2 cloves of garlic

1/4 cup olive oil

Sauté eggplant, zucchini, onions & peppers together in olive oil. Mix in all remaining ingredients and let simmer on low until eggplant is fully cooked.

Layer pasta sheets in bottom of casserole dish, add vegetables and layer another of the pasta sheets and vegetables, leaving the top layer pasta.

Sprinkle the cheese and bake in a 350 degree oven for 25 minutes.

Shrimp and Scallops with Spinach Flan

Serves 6

1/2 cup heavy cream

12 scallops (10 count)

24 shrimp (13-15 count)

3 teaspoons paprika

1/2 cup olive oil

1/4 pound fresh sorrel

2 cups fish stock

1/4 cup roux

6 bamboo skewers

In a bowl, mix shrimp, scallops, paprika and olive oil; salt & pepper to taste.

Bring to a boil the fish stock, add roux to thicken and then add cream.

Put 4 shrimp and 2 scallops on each skewer.

Julienne sorrel leaves, slice thinly and sauté until cooked.

Add to the sauce. Cook the scallops and shrimp until done.

Spinach Flan

2 ounces butter
1/2 quart heavy cream
1/2 quart half & half
1 pound bag of spinach
1/4 teaspoon nutmeg
6 whole eggs

Cook the spinach in butter for 5 minutes, let cool. Mix the spinach with the cream, half & half and egg. Coarsely chop the spinach and add to cream mixture.

Add nutmeg and salt and pepper to taste.

Put the mixture into 4 ounce aluminum cups and bake at 350 degrees for 27 minutes.

Seafood Galette

Yield: 8 servings
8 ounces grouper
salt and pepper to taste
2 egg whites
4 cups heavy cream, divided
1/2 ounce (1 tablespoon) Dijon mustard
6 drops hot sauce
8 drops Worcestershire sauce
2 tablespoons chopped chives
1 tablespoon chopped cilantro
4 ounces lobster, chopped
8 ounces each: salmon, shrimp, crab meat, chopped
melted butter for ring molds
olive oil for sautéing
3 shallots, finely chopped
2 tablespoons red-wine vinegar
2 cups white wine
chopped tarragon to taste
14 ounces unsalted butter

Heat oven to 350 degrees. Cube grouper. Place in the work bowl of
a food processor. Add salt and freshly ground pepper to taste.
Process until smooth.
Add egg whites. Process until well incorporated.
With the machine running, add 3 cups cream in a steady stream.
Add grouper mixture to mixing bowl.
Add mustard, hot sauce, Worcestershire sauce, chives and cilantro.
Add chopped salmon, lobster, shrimp and crab meat. Butter 8
(6-ounce) ring molds.
Fill with seafood mixture. Bake 20 minutes.

Sauté shallots in butter. Add red wine vinegar, white wine and chopped tarragon to a sauté pan. Let cook until reduced in volume by two-thirds.

Add 1 cup heavy cream and bring to a boil.

Let reduce in volume to half. Add salt and pepper to taste.

With mixture simmering, add butter in small pieces. Using a hand-held mixer, whip the sauce right in the pan to give the mixture a smooth, white, foamy consistency.

Heat olive oil in a sauté pan.

Pan fry baked Galettes until golden on both sides. Place Galettes on plates.

Add sauce. Garnish as desired.

Chocolate Mousse

4 1/2 ounces semi-sweet chocolate
1/3 cup butter, broke into pieces
2 egg yolks
3 egg whites
1 1/2 tablespoons granulated sugar
Melt the chocolate in a double boiler.
Remove from heat and add the butter, stirring with a wooden spoon.
Add the egg yolks and mix in.
Allow the mixture to cool completely.
Beat the egg whites until very stiff; halfway through, add the sugar.
Fold the egg whites into the chocolate mixture, beginning with a handful to soften the chocolate.
Gently fold in the remainder with a spatula.
Place in a dish and refrigerate for at least 2 hours to set.
Garnish as desired.

Beef Fillets

4 (8 oz.) beef fillets, trimmed
1 tablespoon butter
1 tablespoon olive oil
3 tablespoons freshly ground black pepper
salt
6 tablespoons brandy
3/4 cup dry red wine
1 shallot, chopped
1 1/2 cups veal or beef stock or broth
1 tablespoon butter

Heat the butter and olive oil in a skillet. Dip the fillets in black pepper and season with salt.
Panfry, turning once to evenly brown, until cooked as desired.
Add brandy and flambé.
Remove fillets and cover loosely with foil.
Add the wine and shallots to skillet and sauté 5 minutes. Add stock & remaining butter and cook 3 minutes, until slightly thickened.
Serve sauce over fillets.

Goat Cheese Salad
Fried Cheese

goat cheese
egg wash
bread crumbs
Dip goat cheese slices in egg wash and then coat with bread crumbs;
fry in pan until warm.

Salad

mixed field greens
arugula
grapes
grape tomatoes
walnuts

Vinaigrette

Mix together the following ingredients:
1 tablespoon French mustard
2 tablespoons red wine vinegar
1 ounce salt
1/2 ounce pepper
1 egg
Then slowly add 10 tablespoons of oil.

Baked French Onion Soup

Yields: 4-6 servings

1 1/2 pounds yellow onions, diced

1/2 cup (1 stick) unsalted butter

2 tablespoons flour

1 1/2 teaspoon salt

1/2 teaspoon ground black pepper

2 teaspoons dried (or 2 fresh sprigs) thyme

2 tablespoons dried (or 2 fresh sprigs) parsley

2 dried bay leaves

2 1/2 quarts chicken broth

9 ounces Gruyere cheese, grated

1 French bread loaf

Melt butter in large pot.

Add diced onions and sauté over medium heat until translucent and caramelized.

Add flour and stir until a blonde roux forms.

Pour in chicken broth, stir well. Add herbs, salt and pepper.

Bring to a boil then reduce heat to low and cover pot with lid.

Let simmer for 20-30 minutes.

Ladle soup into oven-proof bowls or ramekins and top with grated Gruyere cheese.

Place under broiler until cheese is melted and lightly browned.

Served with slices of oven-toasted French bread

Lobster Bisque

14 ounces raw lobster in the shell
1/3 cup butter
1 medium onion, chopped
2 shallots, finely chopped
1/4 clove of garlic, crushed
4 cups fish stock
4 whole black peppercorns
2 1/2 cups water
1/3 cup flour
1 3/4 cups tomato puree
2 tablespoons cognac
1/2 cup heavy cream
1 teaspoon each: chervil & tarragon

Melt half the butter in a pan, add the onions and cook until softened, when done add the garlic and shallots, cook briefly. Add the lobster, fish stock, peppercorns and the water. Bring to a boil, reduce the heat and simmer for 20 minutes.

Remove the lobster from the stock, cool and take the meat from the shells and set aside. Crush the shells and return to the pan and continue to simmer for 40 minutes.

Strain the stock through a sieve.

In a blender, puree the lobster with some of the stock.

Mix the flour and remaining butter to make a paste.

Add paste, tomato puree, cognac, cream, and mix well, salt and pepper to taste. Add the tarragon and chervil cook, stirring continuously over high heat until the soup thickens.

Reduce and simmer gently for 5 minutes.

Croque Monsieur

2 tablespoons minced shallots

2 to 3 tablespoons butter or margarine, at room temperature

1 tablespoon all-purpose flour

1/4 cup chicken broth

1/4 cup milk or whipping cream

6 ounces gruyère cheese, shredded

4 slices of Gruyère cheese, thickly sliced

1/16 teaspoon fresh grated or ground nutmeg

8 slices firm white bread, thickly sliced

1/4 pound sliced cooked ham

shredded provolone, parmesan and Swiss mixed together

In a large nonstick frying pan over medium-high heat, stir shallots in 1 tablespoon butter.

Stir often until golden, about 3 minutes.

Add flour; stir until blended. Remove from heat and add broth and milk; whisk to blend well. Return to heat and whisk until mixture is boiling vigorously.

Remove from heat and add cheese and nutmeg; stir until cheese is melted.

Pour sauce into a bowl.

Lightly butter one side of each bread slice and lay buttered sides down on a sheet pan.

Divide half the cheese sauce equally among 4 slices; spread sauce to edges.

Lay ham, cheese equally over sauce, top with the remaining bread slices.

Place the provolone, parmesan and Swiss cheese on top of the bread and bake in the oven until cheese is melted

Gratin de Macaroni

Pasta with Gruyere and Parmesan Cheeses

Yield: 4 servings
3/4 pound pasta
3 cups whole milk
4 tablespoons unsalted butter
1/3 cup flour
1 pinch nutmeg
1/2 cup heavy cream
1 1/2 cups shredded Gruyère cheese
2 tablespoons freshly grated Parmesan cheese
coarse salt and freshly ground black pepper, to taste
Preheat oven to 400 degrees.
Butter a large baking dish; set aside.
Begin cooking the pasta until just al dente, or slightly underdone.
(*Keep a close eye on your pasta while you cook the sauce - you would
not want to overcook it!*)
Drain and set aside when done.
While the pasta cooks, heat milk in a small saucepan over medium
heat - do not let simmer. Melt butter in a medium saucepan. Add
flour to melted butter. Stir 1 to 2 minutes, until butter-flour mixture
is golden. Slowly whisk in warm milk. Add nutmeg, salt, and
pepper.
Cook sauce, whisking often, until thickened, about 10 minutes.
Remove from heat.
Add heavy cream and half of the Gruyère cheese. Stir until cheese is
completely melted. Combine the pasta with the cheese sauce.
Pour the pasta and cheese into the large baking dish.

Top with remaining half of Gruyère and Parmesan.

Cover dish with foil.

Bake 10 minutes. Remove foil and continue baking until cheese is golden brown.

Remove from oven and let cool for at least 10 minutes before serving.

Crème Brulee

Yield: 7 servings
8 egg yolks
1 cup half and half
3 cups heavy cream
1 cup granulated sugar
1 vanilla bean
brown sugar
Whisk the eggs with sugar until blended, incorporate the half and half and cream.
Mix in the vanilla bean and refrigerate overnight.
Heat oven to 200 degrees
Remove vanilla bean, pour mixture into individual baking dishes, place them on a sheet pan of water (*so the crème Brulee won't burn*), and cover with another pan on top of the baking dishes.
Bake 1 1/2 hours.
Remove from oven and chill.
Sprinkle a layer of brown sugar on top the crème Brulee and broil until melted and caramelized.
Cool and serve.

Beef Short Ribs

4 pounds beef ribs

Marinade

2 cups cabernet wine
3 sprigs rosemary
3 sprigs thyme
1 whole garlic bulb with head cut off
pearl onions
button mushrooms
1 teaspoon black peppercorns
salt and pepper
Marinate the ribs for 12 hours, place the marinade and ribs in an oven safe dish, slowly cook for 2 1/2 hours at 300 degrees until tender.

The International Gateway

As you leave the France Pavilion you will come upon the International Gateway entrance to the park.

Tucked away in a quite space between France and the United Kingdom is Epcot's International Gateway, the "less hectic" secondary entrance and exit for the park.

This lesser-known entrance to the park opened in 1990 just before Disney's Swan Hotel opened. The Gateway was planned so that guests of the soon-to-be opened Epcot Area deluxe resorts (Yacht Club, Beach Club, Boardwalk Inn, and the non-Disney Swan and Dolphin) would have an "exclusive" back door entrance to the park, much like the Monorail provided to guests at the Magic Kingdom deluxe resorts.

And so the International Gateway was built providing the guests with an entrance gate to the park in addition to a completed waterway going all the way to Disney's Hollywood Studios (MGM Studios at the time). The new waterway also meant the fleet of

Friendship boats would be expanded to provide guests another transportation option to get to the resorts and the Studios.

But there's more to the International Gateway than just an entrance and exit for guests at the resorts.

If you take a stroll down the pathway that leads to the entrance/exit gate and the Friendship Boats you'll find a gift shop called World Traveler.

The World Traveler shop is decorated with travel posters, giving it an international flair. Guests will find the usual suspects when it comes to Disney souvenirs, but on a few occasions we've also found some unique items that we didn't see anywhere else.

The store is rather small inside, but if you're headed out of the park and need something quick it's a good place to stop. You'll also find essentials including sunscreen, cool drinks, and even "umbrella" style strollers, all of which might come in handy as you walk back to your resort.

Another thing you might find outside World Traveler is characters ready to meet-and-greet guests. And sometimes, they are characters you don't expect to meet in Epcot.

Among them are Goofy's son Max and Captain Hook.

Another fun bit of trivia: If you stand in the France pavilion and look across the "Seine" you'll notice that the gateway resembles the buildings in France. This was intentional as it needed to compliment the buildings in France.

Restrooms are located just before the entrance at the International Gateway, and there is also a ticket booth. The dock for the Friendship Boats is located before the entrance to the Gateway and guests arriving on the boats have a short walk to Epcot.

Guests arriving to the International Gateway will go through bag check just as they would at the main entrance. Strollers, wheelchairs, and some ECV's can be rented once guests go through the entrance. There is also a locker rental area just inside the gates.

The International Gateway is definitely a perk when you're staying in the Epcot resort area. Guests can avoid the hustle and bustle of the main entrance of Epcot in the morning (after enjoying a leisurely walk from their hotel), and they also have a "quick getaway" after Illuminations fireworks ends.

The United Kingdom Pavilion

The United Kingdom Pavilion is the bump in the road between the Le Cellier (Canada) and the Chef's de France. There are some beautiful buildings here and even some great food.

There aren't any rides, shows, or movies here. But there is a maze made with a hedge. There are a couple of places to grab a pint and rest your weary feet while you enjoy your drink.

The buildings here are a hodgepodge of architectural styles from different periods ranging from 1500 to 1800 AD.

The pavilion opened in 1982 along with the rest of Epcot. This area drips with hundreds of years of history. The building styles represented is Victorian, London, Yorkshire Manor, Tudor, Georgian, Hyde Park, and Regency and there's even a Shakespearean cottage. Over 500 years of construction history are on display.

The Food

The amazing food and drinks are the draws here.

Rose and Crown Pub is a traditional, English pub. Not only can you find all kinds of drinks, they serve some very good English food like **Fish n Chips**

If you want something quick and good check out Yorkshire County Fish Shop. This unobtrusive little joint features great fish and chips.

Magical Star Cocktail

1 part X Rated Fusion Liqueur
1 part Parrot Bay Coconut Rum
3 parts pineapple juice
1 part souvenir multicolored glow cube

English Rose

2 parts gin
2 parts apricot brandy
1 part sweet vermouth
2 parts orange juice
1 part pineapple juice
1 part cranberry juice

Leaping Leprechaun

1 part rum
1 part vodka
1 part Midori
2 parts sweet and sour
3 parts Sprite

Welsh Dragon

1 part peach schnapps
1 part Midori
1 part crème de menthe
3 parts orange juice
2 parts pineapple juice
Mix all ingredients together, blending well. Pour over ice.

English Rose Cocktail

1 oz gin
1 oz apricot brandy
.5 oz sweet vermouth
1 oz orange juice
.5 oz pineapple juice
.5 oz cranberry juice

Lemon Posset

Yield: 4 servings

16 ounces heavy cream
4 ounces powdered sugar
juice of three lemons

Topping

1/2 pint fresh raspberries
1/2 pint fresh strawberries
3 ounces corn syrup
1 ounce orange juice
Bring heavy cream to a boil, then add sugar. Reduce for four
minutes. Add the lemon juice, mix well and keep cooking for 2
more minutes.
Pour the mixture into a glass or bowl and put it into the refrigerator
overnight.
Mixture should be firm.
Topping: Mix corn syrup with orange juice, and then add berries.
Garnish with fresh berries and serve.

Bangers and Mash with Onion Gravy

yields 4 servings
4 links pork sausage
2 pounds potatoes, peeled and cubed
1/4 cup butter
1 tablespoon butter
2 tablespoons milk (optional)
0.5 Gal Whole Milk
1 teaspoon dry mustard powder
salt and ground black pepper to taste
1 tablespoon butter
2 large onions, chopped
6 cups beef broth
2 cups red wine
Preheat oven to 200 degrees F

Cook the sausage links in a skillet over medium-low heat until
browned on all sides, about 5 minutes per side; transfer to an
oven-safe dish and move to the preheated oven to keep warm.

Place potatoes into a saucepan over medium heat, cover with water,
and boil gently until potatoes are tender, 10 to 15 minutes.

Drain and allow to steam dry for a minute or two.

Mix in 1/4 cup of butter, milk, dry mustard, salt, and black pepper;
mash until fluffy and smooth.

Set aside.

Melt 1 tablespoon butter in a skillet over medium-high heat;
Cook the onions until translucent and just starting to brown, about
8 minutes.

Pour in the beef broth and red wine; boil the mixture down to
about half its volume, about 10 minutes.

Season with salt and black pepper.

To serve, place a sausage onto a serving plate with about 1/2 cup of mashed potatoes.

Pour the onion gravy over the sausage and potatoes.

Pot Roast

Salt and freshly ground black pepper
One 3- to 5-pound chuck roast
2 or 3 tablespoons olive oil
2 whole onions, peeled and halved
6 to 8 whole carrots, unpeeled, cut into 2-inch pieces
1 cup red wine, optional
3 cups beef broth
2 or 3 sprigs fresh rosemary
2 or 3 sprigs fresh thyme
Preheat the oven to 275 degrees F.
Generously salt and pepper the chuck roast.
Heat the olive oil in large pot or Dutch oven over medium-high heat.
Add the halved onions to the pot, browning them on both sides.
Remove the onions to a plate.
Throw the carrots into the same very hot pot and toss them around a bit until slightly browned, about a minute or so. Reserve the carrots with the onions.
If needed, add a bit more olive oil to the very hot pot. Place the meat in the pot and sear it for about a minute on all sides until it is nice and brown all over.
Remove the roast to a plate.
With the burner still on high, use either red wine or beef broth (about 1 cup) to deglaze the pot, scraping the bottom with a whisk.
Place the roast back into the pot and add enough beef stock to cover the meat halfway.
Add in the onions and the carrots, along with the fresh herbs.
Put the lid on, and then roast for 3 hours for a 3-pound roast.
For a 4 to 5-pound roast, plan on 4 hours.
The roast is ready when it's fall-apart tender.

Corned Beef and Cabbage

This recipe takes 10 days of preparation

Yield: 6 to 8 servings

2 to 2 1/2 pound Corned-Beef Brisket*, recipe follows

1 tablespoon coarsely ground black pepper

1 teaspoon ground allspice

2 bay leaves

2 teaspoons kosher salt

1/2 pound diced carrots, approximately 4 small

1/2 pound diced onions, approximately 2 small

1 pound potatoes, peeled and chopped, approximately 3 medium

1/4 pound diced celery, approximately 2 stalks

1 small head cabbage, chopped, approximately 2 pounds

Corned Beef

2 quarts water
1 cup kosher salt
1/2 cup brown sugar
2 tablespoons saltpeter
1 cinnamon stick, broken into several pieces
1 teaspoon mustard seeds
1 teaspoon black peppercorns
8 whole cloves
8 whole allspice berries
12 whole juniper berries
2 bay leaves, crumbled
1/2 teaspoon ground ginger
2 pounds ice
1 (4 to 5 pound) beef brisket, trimmed
1 small onion, quartered
1 large carrot, coarsely chopped
1 stalk celery, coarsely chopped

*Cook's note: Brisket should be prepared through the brining stage, but not cooked.

Place the water into a large 6 to 8 quart stockpot along with salt, sugar, saltpeter, cinnamon stick, mustard seeds, peppercorns, cloves, allspice, juniper berries, bay leaves and ginger.

Cook over high heat until the salt and sugar have dissolved.

Remove from the heat and add the ice.

Stir until the ice has melted.

If necessary, place the brine into the refrigerator until it reaches a temperature of 45 degrees F.

Once it has cooled, place the brisket in a 2-gallon zip top bag and add the brine. Seal and lay flat inside a container, cover and place in the refrigerator for 10 days.

Check daily to make sure the beef is completely submerged and stir the brine.

After 10 days, remove from the brine and rinse well under cool water.

Place the brisket into a pot just large enough to hold the meat, add the onion, carrot and celery and cover with water by 1-inch.

Set over high heat and bring to a boil.

Reduce the heat to low, cover and gently simmer for 2 1/2 to 3 hours or until the meat is fork tender.

Remove from the pot and thinly slice across the grain.

Place the corned beef, pepper, allspice, bay leaves and salt into a large 8-quart pot along with 3-quarts of water.

Cover and set over high heat.

Bring to a boil, decrease the heat to low and cook, at a low simmer for 2 1/2 hours.

After 2 1/2 hours add the carrots, onions, potatoes and celery.

Return to a simmer and cook uncovered for 15 minutes.

After 15 minutes, add the cabbage and cook for an additional 15 to 20 minutes until the potatoes and cabbage are tender.

Remove the bay leaves and serve immediately.

Red Onion Jam

1 pound red onions, julienne
1 tablespoon canola/olive blend
1/4 cup red wine (Cabernet)
1/4 cup red wine vinegar
1/4 cup balsamic vinegar
1/2 cup sugar, granulated
pinch of kosher salt
Heat pan with oil.
Add onions and sauté until caramelized.
Add sugar and caramelized.
Deglaze with wine and vinegar.
Reduce until syrup-like consistency. Let cool.
Serve with a cheese platter.
Note: Store in refrigerator up to 2 weeks.

Lemon Tart

Short Dough

1/2 pound unsalted butter (2 sticks)
3/4 cup sugar
1/4 teaspoon salt
1 egg
3 1/3 cups pastry flour, sifted

Filling

1 cup lemon juice
5 eggs
2 cups granulated sugar
1 cup butter

Meringue Topping

6 egg whites

1 1/4 cup granulated sugar

Method of preparation for Short Dough: Using the paddle attachment of a stand mixer at low speed, combine the butter, sugar and salt until they're fully mixed.

Add the eggs and keep mixing until incorporated.

Add flour.

Mix until incorporated.

Do not over mix, or mix at a high speed, this will cause the dough to be tough.

Chill the dough for 3 to 4 hours before using.

For Lemon Filling: In a sauce pan, heat up lemon juice, sugar and butter to a boil. Remove from stove. Then add eggs and mix well.

For Meringue Topping: In a double boiler, heat the sugar and the egg whites until warm, whipping constantly with a wire whip.

Transfer the meringue into a bowl using a power mixer and beat on high until very stiff.

Method of assembly: Roll out the dough to 1/8 inch thick, use a 10 inch ring that 1 1/2 inch high, lay the dough on the bottom and sides of pan. Pour in the lemon filling. Bake at 300 degrees for about 15 to 20 minutes until the custard sets.

Take and out oven and let cool.

Put the meringue into a pastry bag and pipe it on the cool lemon tart.

Scotch Barley Soup

Yield: 5 quarts.

1/4 cup butter
1 cup diced white part of leeks
1 cup chopped onion
1 cup diced carrots
1 cup chopped celery
1 cup diced white turnips
1 pound mutton or lamb neck or breast (*or use 1/2 lb. ground lamb*)
2-3 tablespoons all-purpose flour
1 cup pearl barley
4 quarts chicken broth
2-3 tablespoons cornstarch
1 1/2 cup Half and Half
salt and freshly ground pepper to taste

Heat butter in a large saucepan and sauté leeks and onion for 5 minutes.

Add carrots, celery and turnips and continue cooking for 10 minutes. Remove fat and fell from lamb and grind meat in a food processor with the steel blade or a grinder.

(Or buy already ground lamb.)

Add the meat to vegetables and cook and stir to keep meat from lumping, until it is lightly browned.

Sprinkle flour over meat to absorb fat.

Meanwhile, cover barley with boiling water and let stand 10 minutes. Drain and rinse with cold water. Add to vegetables and meat with 1 cup chicken broth.

Cover and let steam over low heat 10 minutes. Add remaining chicken broth and bring to a boil.

Reduce heat and simmer 1 to 1 1/2 hours or until barley is tender.

Blend cornstarch and Half and Half and stir into soup. Let boil
until slightly thickened.

Add salt and pepper to taste.

NOTE: This soup freezes well.

Guinness Stew

Serves 6 - 8

2 pounds sirloin cubes
1/2 cup all-purpose flour
2 tablespoons ounce olive oil
2 dry bay leaves
1 large clove garlic, chopped
1 cup diced yellow onion
1/2 cup diced carrots
1 tablespoon chopped fresh thyme
1 tablespoon chopped fresh rosemary
1/4 teaspoon red chili flakes
1 cup Guinness stout
1 quart (4 cups) beef broth

Place steak and flour in a plastic bag; seal bag and shake vigorously to coat.

Heat oil in a large, heavy-bottomed stockpot;
add steak and cook over medium-high heat until browned, stirring occasionally.

Reserve remaining flour in bag.

Add bay leaves, garlic, onions, and carrots, and cook about 5 minutes, until tender. Sprinkle in remaining flour; cook one minute, stirring constantly. Add the thyme, rosemary, and chili flakes. Slowly stir in Guinness Stout while scraping the bottom of the pan to loosen any particles. Stir until smooth, thickened, and bubbly.

Season with salt and pepper.

Simmer 10 minutes.

Slowly stir in beef broth and bring to a boil.

Cover, reduce heat, and simmer 1 hour.

Stew will thicken and reduce by at least 1/3.

Discard bay leaves before serving.

Cook's note: To thicken stew if wanted, make a slurry of 1 ounce cornstarch and 2 ounces water and add to stew while at a simmer.

Guinness Cake

Yield: 8 servings
1/2 cup unsalted butter
2 1/2 cups brown sugar
6 eggs
2 cups all-purpose flour
1 tablespoon baking powder
1 teaspoon baking soda
2 cups Guinness Stout
1/2 cup cocoa powder

Grease and line a cake pan and preheat oven to 275 degrees.

Cream butter and sugar together. Gradually beat in eggs.

Sift the flour, baking powder, baking soda into a separate bowl.

Stir Guinness into cocoa.

Carefully fold in alternate quantities of flour and cocoa to butter/ sugar mixture.

Spread mixture into pans and bake for 1 hour 30 minutes at 275 degrees.

Let cool in pans for five minutes before turning out.

Crab Appetizer

2 cups lump crab meat
1/4 cup orange juice
1 tablespoon curry powder
1 small red pepper, diced
1 small red onion, diced
1 tablespoon chopped fresh chives
to taste kosher salt
to taste pepper

Make sure the crab as no shell pieces in it. In a bowl, add all ingredients, blending well.

Store in airtight container in the refrigerator.

Season to taste with salt and pepper before serving.

Mushroom Medley

1 tablespoon olive oil
2 tablespoons chopped garlic
4 tablespoons chopped shallots
1 cup button mushrooms, sliced
1 cup shitake mushrooms, sliced
1 cup Portobello mushrooms, sliced
1 cup Crimini mushrooms, sliced
1 cup white wine
2 cups heavy cream
to taste salt
to taste pepper

In a large pot, quickly sweat the shallots and garlic in olive oil.
Add the mushrooms starting with buttons, crimini, portabellas, and the shitakes last allowing three minutes between batches.
Add white wine and simmer for five minutes.
Add heavy cream, bring to a boil and then simmer for 5 minutes to get the correct thickness, making sure it coats the back of a spoon well.
Season with salt and pepper to taste

Potato Leek Soup

Makes 16-18 ounces
6 potatoes
4 quarts heavy cream
1 onion, diced
2 bunches leeks
1/4 cup butter
salt & pepper to taste

Cut up potatoes then place in a container covered with water so they won't turn brown,
then set aside.
Cut off the green tops of the leeks, you just want to use the white part.
Cut up leeks & then place them in water to get the dirt off them.
In a heavy pot, melt the butter & then add the onion and leeks.
Cook them for 5 to 10 minutes.
Add cut up potatoes, then add cream.
Let soup simmer until the potatoes are cooked.
This will vary due to the size of the potatoes.
When the potatoes are cooked, puree soup with a hand blender until smooth.
Then season with salt & pepper.

Sticky Toffee Pudding

12 ounces dates, chopped and blanched
8 ounces hot water
2 teaspoons vanilla bean
2 teaspoons baking soda
1 pound all-purpose flour
2 teaspoons baking powder
4 ounces unsalted butter
12 ounces sugar
2 whole eggs
1/4 teaspoon salt

Chop dates and add to hot water. Stir in vanilla and baking soda.
Cream butter and sugar, then add eggs one at a time.
On low speed add half flour and baking powder and all of the
liquid; mix until combined.
Fold in rest of flour to mixture.
Fill greased molds halfway and bake 15 minutes at 325 degrees.

Butter Rum Toffee Sauce

1 ounce butter
4 ounces heavy cream
3 ounces dark brown sugar
1/2 ounce dark rum
Combine butter, sugar, and cream; bring to a boil.
Remove from heat and add rum. Stir until all is incorporated. Serve hot.

Custard Sauce

8 egg yolks
3 ounces castor sugar
1 vanilla bean
1/2 pint milk
1/2 pint heavy cream

Beat the egg yolks and sugar together in a bowl until well blended.
Scrape the insides of the vanilla pod, if using, into the milk and
cream, add the pod too, and bring to the boil.
Sit the bowl over a pan of hot water and whisk the cream into the
egg yolks and sugar.
As the egg yolks cook, the custard will thicken.
Keep stirring until it starts to coat the back of a spoon, then remove
the bowl from the heat and the pod from the custard.
Serve warm or cold. Stir the sauce occasionally until cool, to prevent
a skin forming, or cover with grease proof paper while it cools.

Fish n Chips

Yield: 6 servings

3 pounds white-flesh fish, boneless (*cod, snapper, haddock, grouper*)

1 cup lemon juice

1 tablespoon Worcestershire sauce

1/4 teaspoon salt

1/4 teaspoon white pepper

2 tablespoons vegetable seasoning

Batter (*recipe follows*)

oil for frying

chips (*French fries*), fresh or frozen, cooked

malt vinegar

Cut fish into fingers about 2 ounces each and place in a glass or stainless steel pan.

Mix lemon juice with Worcestershire sauce, salt, pepper, and vegetable seasoning.

Pour over fish and marinate in refrigerator for 1 hour, turning every so often to coat fish.

Prepare batter. Remove fish from marinade, drain, dip in batter and fry in hot oil for about 5 minutes, turning to brown both sides, if necessary.

Remove from oil and drain on paper towels.

Serve with chips and malt vinegar.

Batter

3/4 cup cornstarch
2 2/3 cups flour
1 teaspoon salt
3 teaspoons sugar
1/8 teaspoon white pepper
1 3/4 cups water
2 egg yolks
1/3 cup flat beer
2 teaspoons baking powder
Mix cornstarch, flour, salt, sugar, and pepper.
In a separate bowl, beat water, egg yolks, and beer together
with a whisk and slowly add dry ingredients.
Continue to mix with whisk until mixture is smooth.
Stir in baking powder.
Makes enough batter to coat 3 pounds of fish

Cottage Pie

Serves: 4
1/4 cup butter
1 cup diced onion
1 1/2 pounds lean ground beef
Salt and freshly ground pepper to taste
1/4 teaspoon ground savory
1 cup brown gravy
2 cups mashed potatoes
additional butter

Heat 1/4 cup butter in a 9-inch skillet. Add onion and cook until lightly browned, stirring.

Add beef, salt, pepper and savory and continue cooking 5 minutes longer.

Stir in gravy and heat until bubbling.

Spoon into a buttered 8 cup flat casserole dish.

Top meat mixture with mashed potatoes.

Dot with pieces of butter.

Bake at 400 degrees for 15 to 20 minutes, or until potatoes are lightly browned.

Citrus Trifle

Yields 4 Servings

2 cups vanilla pudding (*following directions on box*)

1 1/2 teaspoon lemon juice concentrate

1 1/2 teaspoon orange juice concentrate Lady fingers

orange sections

grapefruit sections

4 dessert glasses

Mix the pudding, lemon and orange juice concentrate together.
In your dessert glass, layer the pudding, orange sections, ladyfingers,
pudding, grapefruit sections and ladyfingers.

Chicken and Leek Pie

2 tablespoons butter
1/3 cup onion, diced
1/2 cup celery, cut on bias
1 cup leeks, whites only, cleaned and diced
1 pound chicken breast, boneless, cubed
2 tablespoons flour
1 1/2 cups chicken stock or broth
1/4 cup parsley, chopped
2 teaspoons salt
1/4 teaspoon pepper
1/4 teaspoon thyme
pie crust, enough for a two crust pie
1 egg, beaten

Melt butter in a large skillet. Add onion, celery and leeks.
Sauté until tender (*10 to 15 minutes on medium heat*).
Add cubed chicken meat and continue cooking until chicken is
tender.
Sprinkle with flour and stir well.
Add stock, parsley, salt, pepper and thyme. Bring to a boil and cook
for 3 to 5 minutes.
Remove from heat and let cool slightly.
Preheat oven to 400 degrees. Line a 2 quart casserole dish at least 2
inch deep with pie crust.
Spoon in filling
Top with more crust. Cut hole in top. Brush with egg.
Bake 25 to 30 minutes until crust is golden brown and filling is hot.
Allow pie to rest 10 minutes before serving.

Bailey's Irish Coffee Trifle Custard

1 1/2 cups sugar
3/4 cup cocoa powder
1/2 cup cornstarch
1/8 teaspoon coarse salt
3 cups whole milk
3 cups half-and-half
3 ounces bittersweet chocolate
2 tablespoons vanilla extract
3 ounces coffee

In a mixing bowl, whisk together the sugar, cocoa, cornstarch, and salt.

In a thin stream, whisk in the milk until smooth.

In a thin stream, whisk in the half-and-half until smooth.

Strain the mixture through a fine sieve into a saucepan.

Over medium heat, whisking the mixture constantly, bring to a boil.

Boil gently for 2 minutes.

Turn off the heat and stir in the coffee, bittersweet chocolate and vanilla.

Fill a large bowl with ice cubes, rest the saucepan on top, and add cold water to cover the ice cubes.

Refrigerate until well chilled.

The recipe can be made up to 2 days in advance.

Serve cold.

Chocolate Cake

1 3/4 cups all-purpose flour
1 3/4 cups brown sugar
3/4 cup cocoa
1 1/2 teaspoons baking powder
1 1/2 teaspoons baking soda
1/4 teaspoon salt
1 1/4 cups buttermilk
1 teaspoon vanilla extract
2 eggs
4 tablespoons vegetable oil
1 cup boiling water
Confectioners' sugar
Preheat oven to 350 degrees.

Combine dry ingredients in large bowl and slowly whisk in wet ingredients.
Pour into greased Sheet Pan. Cook for 25 minutes.

Allow to cool.
Cut with a ring mold.

Bailey's Whipped Cream

5 ounces heavy whipped cream
1 ounce Bailey's Irish Cream
Whip Cream until stiff peaks. Fold in Bailey's and pipe on Trifle.

The Canada Pavilion

The Canada Pavilion may be the most beautiful area in all of Walt Disney World. Inside you'll find gardens to walk through, totem poles, a neat movie and the best steak dinner in Epcot.

The beauty of Canada really shines through in every part of this pavilion, except ironically, the entrance to O' Canada (the movie), which is located in a darkish tunnel. Yes, you can look out the windows of the tunnel and see the gardens, but still, it would be a lot more pleasant to wait for the movie outside surrounded by luscious foliage than standing in a drab, dark tunnel.

The Movie

O' Canada is a movie about life in Canada. It's another of those 9 screen surround you with motion; make it look like real life, movies. O Canada is hosted by Martin Short. It shows the diversity of Canadian life. From the hustle bustle of the big cities to the slower lifestyle of the Canadian countryside.

The movie ends with Martin Short inviting you to visit Canada. He says to take a left turn at the big ball and you'll be there soon.

Food

Le Cellier is Epcot's premier steak house. This is the place to visit if you are looking for a big juicy steak. The food here has a Canadian flair. The specialty (aside from steak) is pretzel bread, a Canadian specialty.

The Steaks are big and good and are served with Canadian side dishes like Yukon Potatoes.

Le Cellier is one of the smallest restaurants in Epcot and fills up quickly.

Vodka Martini

Pour a small amount of dry vermouth into a chilled martini glass.
Tilt the glass so the vermouth coats the interior of the glass and
pour out the rest.
Shake the vodka with ice and strain into the prepared glass.
Garnish with a Spanish olive or a lime or lemon twist.

Torontopolitan

5 ounce Chambord
1.5 ounce Iceberg Vodka
.5 ounce Cranberry juice
.5 ounce Orange juice
Mix all ingredients together. Garnish with a cherry.

Eiswein Martini

1 ounce Inniskillan Vidal Eiswein
1 ounce Vodka

Caesar Cocktail

1 part Iceberg Vodka
2 parts Clamato juice
dash of Worcestershire sauce (*Duffy's sauce is the real thing if you can find it*)
dash of Tabasco sauce
pinch of salt and two pinches of ground celery seed.
Stir or shake well and garnish with a stalk of celery.

Wild Mushroom Beef Filet

Serves 4
Steak
4 (8 oz.) beef filets
salt
pepper
olive oil

Truffle Beurre Blanc

1 tablespoon olive oil
1 shallot, sliced
1 cup dry white wine
1 cup heavy cream
1/4 cup cold unsalted butter, cubed
1 tablespoon truffle oil
1/2 lemon, juiced
salt
pepper

Roasted Mushrooms

1/2 lbs. sliced mushrooms
1 shallot, sliced
1/4 cup minced garlic
1/4 olive oil
2 Tbsp. unsalted butter

For the Mushrooms: Preheat oven to 400 degrees. Toss the mushrooms, shallots and garlic in olive oil. Place on a baking sheet and bake for 20 minutes. Melt butter in a saute pan, add the roasted mushrooms and sauté for 3 to 5 minutes.

For the Truffle Beurre Blanc

Heat oil in a medium saucepan; add shallots and cook until
translucent.
Add wine and simmer until reduced by 90% - about 10 minutes.
Add cream and simmer until reduced by 75% - about 12 minutes.
Remove from heat and whisk in butter, a few pieces at a time.
Whisk in truffle oil. Stir in lemon juice, salt and pepper to taste.
Keep warm until ready to serve.

For the Steaks

Grill steaks until desired temperature.

To Serve

Place steak on plate.
Top with mushroom and drizzle with about 2 tablespoons of beurre blanc.

Yukon Potatoes

Yield: 6 servings

3 pounds baby Yukon gold potatoes

Salt

Freshly ground black pepper

3 cups chicken stock

3 tablespoons butter

2 to 3 tablespoons freshly chopped parsley leaves

Place the potatoes in a deep skillet and add salt and pepper, to taste. Cover potatoes halfway with chicken stock, about 3 cups, add the butter and cover skillet with a lid.

Cook the potatoes in the stock until almost tender, about 5 to 8 minutes, depending upon the size of the potatoes. Remove the lid and allow the stock to evaporate, about another 5 minutes.

Once the stock has evaporated pop each potato using a ladle or large spoon, creating a small crack in each, but do not smash.

Allow the potatoes to brown on each side, another 5 minutes, and re-season with salt and pepper, if necessary or desired.

Remove the browned potatoes from the skillet and place onto a serving platter, garnished with the parsley.

Three Onion Soup

Serves 4

1 1/4 cups shallots, sliced

2 1/4 cups Spanish onions, sliced

2 1/4 cups red onions, sliced

2 teaspoons garlic, chopped

1/2 tablespoon olive oil

4 or 5 fresh thyme sprigs, stems removed

1/2 cup good quality dark beer like Guinness

1/2 tablespoon brown sugar

2 1/2 cups beef stock

Heat olive oil over medium heat and add garlic.

Cook slowly and stirring until caramelized (*about 30 minutes*).

Add 1/4 cup of the beer and brown sugar.

Stir to combine. Add stock and fresh thyme.

Cook for 20 minutes simmering over low heat.

Add remaining beer and season to taste with salt and pepper.

Spiced Black Bean Cake

Complete Dish

1 cup Thai Noodle Salad (*recipe below*)
1 red bell pepper
1 teaspoon Arugula Pesto (*recipe below*)
1 cup Black Bean Cake (*recipe below*)
1 slice Pepper jack cheese
1 slice black diamond cheddar

Roast bell pepper over open flame on grill. Peel skin.
Cut pepper in half, stuff with Black Bean Cake mixture.
Top with cheese.
Bake in oven until cheese is melted.
Place noodle salad on plate, serve 2 stuffed pepper halves on top.
Drizzle arugula pesto around plate.

Thai Noodle Salad

1 cup canola oil
1/2 cup chunky peanut butter
1/4 cup soy sauce
1/4 cup sesame oil
1/2 carrot, shredded
1/2 cup sweet chili sauce
2 cups udon noodles, cooked
1 tablespoon chives, chopped fine
Blend peanut butter, soy sauce & chili sauce in a bowl until smooth.
Toss pasta with sauce; add chives and carrots.
Serve immediately.

Arugula Pesto

1/4 cup extra virgin olive oil
3 tablespoons canola oil
1/4 cup fresh arugula, packed tight
1 tablespoon garlic, minced
3 tablespoon Parmesan cheese, grated
1/8 cup pine nuts, toasted
kosher salt and black pepper, to taste

Combine all ingredients except the olive oil in the robot coupe and process well.

On low speed, add the olive oil until fully incorporated.

Adjust seasoning with salt and pepper as/if needed.

Black Bean Cakes

1 can black beans, drained and rinsed
1 chipotle pepper, chopped
1 teaspoon fresh cilantro, chopped
1/4 cup red onion, diced
1/4 cup yellow frozen corn, sliced
1/4 teaspoon Tabasco sauce
1/8 teaspoon chives, julienned
salt and black pepper to taste
Mix all the ingredients together.

Campfire S'mores

Chocolate Brownie, Graham Crackers
and roasted Marshmallows with Vanilla Ice Cream
Serves 12

S'mores Brownie

2 1/2 sticks butter, melted

1 cup cocoa

3 3/4 cups sugar

6 eggs, beaten

1/2 tablespoon vanilla extract

1 3/4 cup flour

1 teaspoon salt

mini marshmallows

cake sprinkles

In a sauce pan, melt butter and add cocoa.

Next add sugar, eggs, and vanilla. Mix well.

Add flour and salt.

Pour into 9 to 13 inch pan over crust (*any store bought graham cracker crust will do*).

Top with mini marshmallows.

Bake at 350 for 30 minutes.

Cut into shapes of your choice, layer with ice cream and fruit sauces.

Skewer marshmallows on a chopstick, burn with a torch (be careful!!) and roll in sprinkles.

Stick through brownie and ice cream.

Smoked Salmon and Crab Timbale

Crab Mascarpone

4 cups of mascarpone cheese
2 cups of Canadian rock crab
1 1/4 cups Old Bay citrus reduction (*recipe below*)
Drain off excess moisture from the crab.
In a bowl, mix all ingredients until well blended by hand.
Mix crab meat in 1/4 of the Old Bay reduction and then press
moisture out again.
Do not overmix or the cheese will break down.

Old Bay Citrus Reduction

1/2 teaspoon lime zest
1/2 teaspoon lemon zest
1 teaspoon orange zest
1/2 cup lemon juice
1/2 cup lime juice
1/4 cup orange juice
1 cup water
1 tablespoon Old Bay Seasoning
3/4 cup powdered sugar
5 tablespoons cornstarch

Zest lime, lemon and orange. Juice each fruit.
Mix fruit juice, water and zest in a heavy sauté pan.
Add Old Bay Seasoning to mixture and heat to a rolling boil.
Add powdered sugar and mix until sauce thickens.
Thicken with cornstarch.

Crab Timbale

2 slices Canadian smoked salmon
1/2 cup crab mascarpone mixture
1 sesame seed cracker
pinch of micro greens
2 tablespoons Old Bay citrus reduction (*recipe above*)
In a stainless steel mold, place one piece of the salmon inside the
bottom of the mold.
Fill the mold with all of the crab mixture.
Place the last piece of salmon on top of the crab mixture and press
down gently.
Place the mold in the middle of a square plate.
Remove the mold from the mixture.
Gently place the micro greens on top of the timbale.
Place the cracker, sharp point into the top of the timbale.
With the remaining sauce, brush 2 lines on the plate.
One in front and one behind the timbale.

Seared Chicken
With Braised Greens and Mustard Jus

Yield: 4 servings

Complete Dish

4 (8-10 oz.) boneless chicken breasts, with the skin on
1/4 cup Lemon Mustard Vinaigrette
4 teaspoons mustard butter
2 cups braised greens
1 cup mustard jus
4 cups cream cheese mashed potatoes

Lemon Mustard Vinaigrette

1 tablespoons Dijon mustard

2 tablespoons grain mustard

1/4 cup lemon juice

1 tablespoon. sherry vinegar

1 clove garlic, minced

1 cup canola oil

to taste salt

to taste pepper

Boil potatoes in salted water until fork tender and drain off water.

Place potatoes on mixing bowl and add in butter and cream cheese
and mash together.

Slowly add in milk to get a creamy texture (*you may not need the full
cup*).

Season the mashed potatoes with salt and pepper to taste.

Braised Greens

2 large bunches of mustard greens, rough chopped and washed
1 medium Spanish onion, small diced
1/2 cup bacon, small diced
3/4 cup chicken broth
to taste salt
to taste pepper
In large soup pot render the bacon until crispy.
Add in the onion and sauté until translucent.
Next add in the mustard greens and the chicken broth and simmer
for 20 to 30 minutes or until greens are tender. When greens are
done adjust seasoning with salt and pepper.

Mustard Jus

2 cups chicken broth
1 teaspoon Dijon mustard
1 teaspoon grain mustard
to taste salt
to taste pepper
Add all ingredients together in small pot and bring to a simmer.
Adjust seasoning with salt and pepper.

Mustard Butter

1/2 cup unsalted butter, soften at room temperature
1 teaspoon Dijon mustard
1 teaspoon grain mustard
3 dashes Tabasco sauce
2 dashes Worcestershire sauce
to taste salt
to taste pepper

Combine all ingredients together in small bowl and whisk together. Adjust seasoning with salt and pepper.

Assembly: The lemon mustard vinaigrette is used to marinate the chicken for 24 hours.

Remove chicken from marinade and sear in lightly oiled cast iron skillet until light brown.

Finish cooking the chicken in a 400 degree oven until it reaches an internal temperature of 165 degrees.

While chicken is in the oven, you should be finishing up your mashed potatoes,
braised greens, and mustard jus.

Place mashed potatoes in serving bowl and top with braised greens. Pour small amount of mustard jus around edge of potatoes and greens.

When the chicken is finished brush with the mustard butter and serve immediately.

Seared Beef Medallions

With Watercress Salad, Cream Cheese Mashed Potatoes

and Vidalia Onion Broth

8 (2-3 oz.) beef tenderloin medallions
1 tablespoon canola oil
1/4 cup Herb Vinaigrette (*recipe follows*)
1 batch Watercress Salad (*recipe follows*)
1 batch Cream Cheese Mashed Potatoes (*recipe follows*)
1 batch Roasted Vidalia Onion Broth (*recipe follows*)
kosher salt to taste
black pepper to taste

Place a heavy skillet or a cast iron skillet over medium high heat.

Season the beef tenderloins with salt and pepper.

Add the canola oil to the skillet. Sear the beef to medium rare, or 2 to 3 minutes per side.

When the meat is finished cooking, place on a plate until service.

To Assemble

Add a scoop of mashed potatoes to the center of a pasta style bowl. Make the watercress salad with the herb vinaigrette, and place on top of potatoes. Place beef on top of the salad. Finish plate with the Roasted Vidalia Onion Broth. (*This means to pour the broth around the base of the potatoes*).

Herb Vinaigrette

1 shallot, finely minced
1 garlic clove, finely minced
1 teaspoon chives, finely chopped
1 teaspoon parsley, finely chopped
1/2 teaspoon picked thyme
1/2 teaspoon rosemary, finely chopped
1/4 cup white balsamic vinegar
2 tablespoons white wine (*Sauvignon Blanc*)
2/3 cup extra virgin olive oil
kosher salt to taste
black pepper to taste

In a saucepan, bring shallots, garlic, thyme, rosemary, and vinegar to a boil.
Boil for one minute then remove from heat. Pulse blend with a hand blender.
Allow to cool to room temperature. Add the wine, chives, parsley, oil, salt and pepper.
Whisk all together to blend well.
Adjust the seasoning with salt and pepper as needed.

Watercress Salad

1 cup watercress, washed and dried
1/2 cup arugula, washed and dried
1/2 cup red pepper, julienne
1/2 cup red onion, julienne
1/2 cup Herb Vinaigrette (*see recipe*)
kosher salt to taste
pepper to taste

Just prior to service, add all ingredients into a medium sized mixing bowl.

Season with salt and pepper. Mix well to coat with the herb vinaigrette.

Cream Cheese Mashed Potatoes

2 lbs. Idaho potatoes, peeled and diced

1/2 stick unsalted butter, room temperature

1/2 cup whole milk, warm

2/3 cup cream cheese, room temperature

kosher salt to taste

black pepper to taste

Place the diced potatoes in a medium saucepan and cover with cold water.

Add about 1 tablespoon of kosher salt.

Boil the potatoes over medium high heat until just tender and cooked through.

Drain water from potatoes.

Process the cooked potatoes in a ricer or a food mill over a bowl that contains the butter and cream cheese.

When finished, add the warm milk and fold together with a wooden spoon or rubber spatula to mix well.

Make sure butter and cheese is fully melted.

Add salt and pepper to taste. Reserve warm for service.

Roasted Vidalia Onion Broth

3 pounds Vidalia onions, peeled and cut in half
1 pound whole shallots, peeled
2 sprigs of thyme
1/4 cup pure olive oil
1/2 gallon chicken stock or broth
kosher salt to taste
pepper to taste

In a large mixing bowl, toss the Vidalia onions, shallots, thyme and olive oil together to coat. Place these ingredients on a cookie sheet and roast in a 400 degree oven for 30 to 45 minutes or until the onions and shallots start to turn brown and caramelize.

Once onions and shallots are dark brown and tender, place all of the roasting ingredients into a stock pot and cover with the chicken stock or broth.

Bring to a light simmer for 45 minutes.

Pull from the heat and puree with a hand blender well.

Place back on the heat and reduce by about half.

Remove the sauce and strain well.

Adjust the seasoning with salt and pepper.

Keep warm for service.

A note: While all these are extraordinary together, they are each worthwhile in their own right.

This salad is a delight anytime you need a salad.

This salad dressing is great with any simple salad.

The onion broth will bring any beef dish to life.

Prince Edward Island Mussels Chowder Style

Yields: 1 portion

1 tablespoon olive oil
1/8 cup apple wood smoked bacon, small dice
1/2 shallot, peeled and sliced
1 small clove garlic, finely minced
1/4 cup russet potatoes, small dice, blanched
1/2 cup heavy cream
1 teaspoon fresh cilantro, rough chop
1/2 pound Prince Edward Island Mussels, washed and scrubbed, beards removed
fresh ground black pepper to taste
kosher salt to taste

Begin the dish by preparing all of the ingredients and set aside.

Place a medium sized sauté pan over medium heat and add the olive oil.

Into the hot oil, place the bacon and cook for 5 to 7 minutes or until bacon fat is rendered and it becomes crispy.

Add the garlic and shallots and continue to sauté for 2 minutes. When the shallots start to become translucent add the potatoes, heavy cream, cilantro, and mussels. Toss all together to blend then cover with a lid or another pan to steam the mussels for about 4 to 5 minutes (*or until all of the mussels open*).

Season with the black pepper and kosher salt

When desired seasoning is obtained, pour into a large soup bowl or pasta dish.

Raspberry Sorbet

2 cups fresh or frozen raspberries
1 cup sugar
1/2 cup water
1 lemon, juiced
1 egg white, optional
To make the raspberry sorbet, puree raspberries and strain through a sieve.
Combine the sugar and water in a saucepan and stir over gentle heat until sugar has dissolved. Turn heat up, and boil for 5 minutes until liquid forms syrup.
Once the syrup has cooled, add the puree and the juice of one lemon.
Freeze in an ice cream maker for 20 minutes.
Alternatively, place mixture in a bowl and put in freezer.
When edges begin to freeze, whisk an egg white, and fold into the partially frozen mixture.
Return to freezer until frozen.

Mashed Sweet Potatoes

Yield: 8 portions

1 pounds Idaho potatoes, peeled
1 pound sweet potato, peeled
1/8 quart unsalted butter
1 cup cream cheese
1 cup milk, warmed
1 tablespoon kosher salt
black pepper to taste

Boil or steam potatoes until tender.
Using a food mill or mixer, incorporate all ingredients together and
adjust seasonings as necessary.

Lemon Mustard Vinaigrette

Yields: 2 cups

1/2 cup lemon juice

2 tablespoons sherry vinegar

2 tablespoons Dijon mustard

2 1/2 tablespoon Creole grain mustard

salt to taste

pepper to taste

1 1/2 cups canola oil

In a bowl, add all ingredients except canola oil.
Add oil in a slow stream to blend.

Roasted Pecan and Roasted Shallot Vinaigrette:

1 1/2 ounces pecans, toasted
3 3/8 ounces roasted shallot puree
2 tablespoons olive oil
1/2 ounce salt
1/8 ounce white pepper
1/4 ounce chopped thyme
1/8 ounce chopped garlic

Toast pecans in 400 degrees oven for about five minutes.
Toss shallots in olive oil with a lot of salt and fresh ground pepper.
Roast in the oven until the outside of the onion begins to caramelize.
Puree in food processor or blender when cool.
Combine all ingredients and adjust the seasoning as needed.

Mixed Field Greens Salad

Yields: 2 cups

Salad

4 cups of ready mixed greens
1/8 cup White Balsamic Vinaigrette (*recipe below*)
4 each poached pear slices (*recipe below*)
1 tablespoon chopped walnuts
1 tablespoon crumbled blue cheese
1/8 cup fresh red beets, peeled and shred (*can use a cheese grater*)
salt and pepper to taste

White Balsamic Vinaigrette

1 tablespoon roasted garlic
1 tablespoon roasted shallots
1/2 cup white balsamic vinegar
1 1/2 cups canola oil
salt and pepper to taste

To Prepare the Vinaigrette

Peel garlic and shallots. Place garlic and shallots on a sheet pan,
sprinkle with 1 tablespoon of the canola oil and cover with foil.
Roast in a 300 degree oven for about 45 minutes or until browned.
Cool. In a blender, add garlic, shallots and vinegar.
Blend well. Add oil in a slow stream to mixture.
Season to taste with salt and pepper.
Store in the refrigerator in an airtight container.

Poached Pears

2 cups water
1 cup sugar
2 pears, peeled and core
1/4 teaspoon cinnamon
1/4 cup red wine vinegar

Preparation for Pears

In a **small** pan, take 2 cups of water and 1 cup sugar and bring to a boil. Peel and core 2 pears. Turn heat down on the sugar mix to low. Add pears, cinnamon, red wine vinegar and cook for 30 to 40 minutes until soft.

Cool in refrigerator. Slice pear for salad garnish.

Presentation of Salad

In a large bowl, toss mixed greens and balsamic vinaigrette.
Add salt and pepper to taste.
Place dressed greens on a large plate and garnish with nuts, cheese,
beets
and sliced poached pears.

Vine Ripened Tomato Stack

1 large vine ripe tomato, thickly sliced
1/2 ounce shallots
1/4 cup spinach, picked, washed and dried
1/4 cup julienne Shiitake mushrooms
2 tablespoons olive oil
2 tablespoons olive oil
1/2 ounce Herb Vinaigrette
drizzle balsamic vinegar- reduced by 1/2
salt and black pepper

Pick and clean spinach. Slice shallots and julienne mushrooms.
In a skillet, add enough olive oil to coat bottom of the pan. Add shallots and sauté till tender.
Add spinach and stir to coat well and wilt the spinach, season to taste with salt and pepper.
Remove from pan and drain. Let cool.
Return pan to heat and coat the skillet with more oil.
Add the shiitake mushrooms and sauté until tender.
Season with salt and pepper.
Remove from pan and allow to cool completely.
Note: These items can be prepared up to one day in advance and held in the refrigerator.
To Assemble Stack: Slice the top and bottom off a large vine ripe tomato. Slice the remaining tomato into 3 slices. Season each slice to taste with salt and pepper. Divide the cooked spinach and mushrooms evenly between the three slices.
Stack the layers on top of each other on a plate.
Drizzle with the Herb Vinaigrette and finish with the balsamic reduction.

Herb Vinaigrette

1/2 cup sliced shallot
2 1/4 cups white balsamic vinegar
1 tablespoon fresh chopped rosemary
1 tablespoon chopped thyme
1 tablespoon minced garlic
1/2 cup Sauvignon Blanc wine
1/8 cup chopped chives
1/8 cup chopped parsley
2 cups extra virgin olive oil
salt and black pepper to taste

Bring shallots, vinegar, rosemary and thyme to a boil. Take off heat. Let completely cool and then add remaining ingredients. Add rest of the ingredients. Whisk together until incorporated, adjust seasoning as needed. Chill, put in container, label, refrigerate. Holds for up to 2 weeks.

Maple Syrup Pie

1/2 cup unsalted butter, melted
4 eggs, lightly beaten
1 cup maple syrup
1 1/2 cups pecan halves
1/2 cup brown sugar, packed firmly
1 (9 inch) pie shell, unbaked
1/8 teaspoon salt
3/4 cup heavy cream, whipped
Preheat oven to 350 degrees.
Blend together butter, maple syrup, brown sugar and salt until mixed well.
Add beaten eggs until incorporated well.
Then add the pecans and mix well.
Pour into the unbaked pie shell. Bake for 40 to 45 minutes until set.
Set on a wire rack to cool.
Serve with vanilla ice cream, lightly whipped cream, or just plain.

Maple Glazed Salmon

Serves 4-6

Candied Pecans

2 ounces pecans, shelled, pieces
2 teaspoons whole butter, unsalted
1 tablespoon apple juice
1/2 tablespoon turbinado sugar (*sugar in the raw*)
pinch kosher salt

Salmon

8 (3 oz.) salmon pieces (*scales removed, skin on*)
2 ounce canola oil
6 ounces cleaned watercress
2 teaspoons extra virgin olive oil
2 ounces candied pecans
8 ounces Maple Glaze
kosher salt
black pepper

Maple Glaze

7 ounces pure maple syrup
1 tablespoon honey, orange blossom
2 tablespoons brown sugar, light
pinch kosher salt
pinch black pepper, fresh ground

Preparation for Pecans

Heat butter in a small saucepan over a medium high heat, until it just starts brown. Immediately add pecans stirring continuously for 5 to 7 minutes until pecans are toasted.

Once pecans have toasted, add apple juice stirring constantly. When nearly all the apple juice has been reduced add the sugar and keep stirring until the pecans have been well coated, take caution not to burn the sugar.

Once pecans are well coated, turn out on to a cooling tray be sure that they are all spaced apart to even cool.

Allow pecans to completely cool in a low humidity environment. Reserve for salmon.

For Glaze

Combine all ingredients in small saucepan and heat over low heat. Heat just long enough to incorporate all ingredients and for sugar to liquefy.

Remove from heat and reserve warm for salmon.

For Salmon

Preheat oven to 425 degrees.

Place watercress in lightly iced water, to rinse and refresh.

Remove from iced water and completely dry in salad spinner or between paper towels, set aside.

Remove any moisture from the salmon pieces by lightly using 1/4 of the canola oil. Season both sides of the salmon with kosher salt and pepper.

Heat remaining 1.5 ounces canola oil in large heavy bottomed non-stick frying pan, large enough to accommodate salmon pieces without overcrowding, over medium high heat.

Ensure that oil is evenly coating bottom of frying pan.

Once the oil has just began to smoke carefully place the salmon pieces in the pan, skin side down, and lower heat to medium.

Cook salmon on skin side until skin is evenly golden brown, turn salmon over and repeat.

Remove salmon from pan and blot on paper towels to remove any oil or fat.

Transfer salmon to baking pan with raised sides, and drizzle each piece with half of the maple glaze, place in oven and bake until desired doneness.

Time will vary depending on the thickness of salmon, average 5 to 10 minutes.

While salmon is baking, toss watercress with olive oil and a pinch of salt and pepper.

Arrange watercress on four plates.

When salmon is done place two pieces on each mound of watercress, drizzle with maple glazed and sprinkle with pecans.

Crab Flan

Crab Flan

5 egg yolks
2 cups heavy cream
1/4 cup charred corn
1 cup crab meat
1/4 teaspoon chopped tarragon
2 tablespoons lemon juice
2 tablespoons small diced red pepper
1 teaspoon Old Bay Seasoning

Mustard Aioli

4 egg yolks
1/2 cup canola oil
8 tablespoon maile mustard
2 tablespoon lemon juice
1 cup chicken stock
salt and pepper to taste

Paprika Aioli

1 egg yolk
1/4 cup canola oil
1/2 cup paprika oil
2 tablespoon maile mustard
2 tablespoons lemon juice
1 tablespoon chicken stock
salt and pepper to taste

Corn Salad

1/4 cup charred corn
1/4 cup diced red pepper
1 teaspoon chopped chives
salt and pepper to taste

Cornbread Crunch

1 cup cornbread crumbs
1 1/2 cups Panko bread crumbs
1 tablespoon crushed red pepper
salt and pepper to taste

Crab Flan

In a large bowl, mix eggs and cream.
Season with salt and pepper.
Add remaining ingredients.
Spoon crab mixture in ramekin dishes sprayed with cooking oil.
Place on cookie sheet. Fill ½ up with water.
Bake at 300 degrees for about 30 minutes or until set.
Let cook and pop out of dish.

For Mustard Aioli

In a small bowl, make an emulsion with egg and canola oil.
Add mustard, lemon juice and stock.
Season with salt and pepper.

For Paprika Aioli

In a small bowl, make an emulsion with the egg yolk, canola oil and
paprika oil.
Add mustard, lemon juice and chicken stock.
Season with salt and pepper.

For Corn Salad

Take an ear of corn, leaving the husk on, grill the corn.
Cut corn off ear. Add chives and salt to taste.

For Corn Bread Crunch

In a small bowl, mix all ingredients.

Assembly

Place 3 crab flan on long thin plate. Drizzle 1 tablespoon mustard aioli over plate. Drizzle 1 tablespoon paprika aioli over plate. Sprinkle cornbread crunch over flan. Sprinkle corn salad over plate.

Crab Cakes

Yields: 10 servings

3 1/4 pounds rock crab meat, picked clean
3/4 cup red and yellow bell peppers , fine dice
1/3 cup leeks, fine dice
3 1/4 tablespoons roasted garlic puree
3 1/4 tablespoons chives, fine cut
3/8 cup mayonnaise
1 5/8 tablespoons chervil, fine dice
3/8 teaspoon cayenne pepper
3/4 ounce fresh lemon juice
1 dash Worcestershire sauce
bread crumbs, as needed
freshly ground black pepper to taste
1 5/8 ounces pasteurized egg yolks

Squeeze liquid from crab meat and pick clean.
Combine garlic, mayonnaise, lemon juice, Worcestershire sauce, and chervil together, add to crab meat.
Fold together. Add remaining ingredients, fold together thoroughly.
Test crab cake (cook one) adjust bread crumbs as necessary, only as a binder, not to be used as a filler.

Chocolate Whiskey Cake

1 cake (*your favorite recipe*)
24 ounces Chocolate Mousse Batch (*recipe below*)
6 ounces Ganache (*recipe below*)
8 ounces Whiskey Syrup (*recipe below*)
Cut your round cake into 3 layers.
Take each layer and drizzle whiskey syrup over each, covering generously.
After whiskey syrup soaks in, cover each layer with chocolate mousse,
and stack all layers together.
Cover completed cake with mousse and decorate with Ganache for icing using a pastry bag with a star tip.

Ganache

1 pound chocolate disks
1/2 quart heavy cream
Heat cream. Do not scald.
Remove from heat and stir in Chocolate Coins until smooth.

Chocolate Mousse Batch

4 1/2 ounces powdered sugar

1/2 quart whipping cream, whipped

7 fluid ounces egg yolk, pasteurized

12 ounces chocolate coins (*or other high quality chopped chocolate*)

Whip eggs and sugar until light and fluffy.

Carefully melt the chocolate over double-boiler steam bath stirring often.

Fold the melted chocolate into the egg and sugar mixture.

Then fold the whipped cream into the chocolate mixture.

Place in the cooler to chill, then portion and serve.

Whiskey Syrup

3/4 quart water
1/2 pound sugar
6 ounces Canadian Club Whiskey
Combine water and sugar in a saucepan. Bring to a boil; stir until all
Sugar is dissolved.
Remove from heat, add the whiskey.

Coffee Crust Dry Rub – Kansas Steak

Yield: 1 cup
1 cup used coffee grounds
1 tablespoon kosher salt
1 teaspoon sugar
1 teaspoon black pepper
1 teaspoon granulated garlic
1. Mix all ingredients together in a bowl.
2. Coat steak on both sides with dry rub before grilling.

Prime Rib with Roasted Potatoes, Au Jus and

Horseradish Cream Sauce

12 ounces prime rib
1 ounces Veal Gemi-Glaze

Veal Demi-Glaze

3 pounds of veal bones

3/4 pound of pig's feet

1/2 carrot, chopped

1 small onion, chopped

1 celery stalk, chopped

1/4 cup finely chopped shallots (*about 1*)

2 garlic cloves, finely chopped

1/4 cup red wine

1 small can tomato paste

1 sprig rosemary

1 sprig thyme

1 whole bay leaf

1 whole peppercorn

2 quarts water

Roast bones in a 350 degree oven for about 1 hour. Spread with tomato paste.

Wrap rosemary, thyme, bay leaf and peppercorn in a piece of cheesecloth.

Deglaze pans with red wine and add all other ingredients in a large pot.

Simmer for 2 to 3 hours.

Remove cheesecloth. Remove and discard bones.

Reserve liquid. Use gravy separator to skim fat (*or let cool, then refrigerate until fat has solidified, at least 2 hours and lift off and discard fat*).

Thicken with cornstarch.

Salt and pepper to taste

Cook prime rib to your liking.

Add 1 ounce of veal demi-glaze

Truffle Beurre Blanc

1 shallot, sliced
1 teaspoon olive oil
1 cup white wine
1 cup heavy cream
1 ounce truffle oil
1/4 cup butter, cubed
juice of 1 lemon
kosher salt to taste
pepper to taste
1 tablespoon chives, minced fine

Saute shallots in the olive oil until translucent. Add wine and vinegar and reduce by 90 percent. Add the cream and reduce by 75 percent.

Remove from heat, and whip in the butter and truffle oil.

Season with salt and pepper and then add lemon juice to taste.

Strain

Stir in chives and keep warm.

Mushroom Risotto

1/2 pound mushrooms, roasted
4 tablespoons olive oil
2 tablespoons minced garlic
to taste kosher salt
to taste fresh cracked black pepper
4 tablespoons whole butter
1 small onion
1 pound Arborio rice
7 cups beef stock
2 cups heavy cream
1 1/2 cups grated Parmesan cheese

Clean mushrooms and toss with enough olive oil just to coat.
Add the minced garlic and season with salt and pepper
Place on parchment lined sheet pan and roast in 375 oven for 20 minutes.
Set aside
In a deep six quart, heavy pan, melt 2 to 3 tablespoons of butter over medium low heat.
Sauté the onions, seasoning with salt and pepper, until soft and clear.
Raise the heat to medium and add the rice
Cook for about three minutes, stirring frequently until it looks chalky and a white dot is clearly visible in the center of each grain.
Meanwhile, bring your beef stock to a simmer.
Heat the cream and keep it on low to keep it warm
Begin to add the beef stock one cup at a time, simmering and stirring until each addition has been absorbed by the rice before adding the next.
After all of the beef stock has been added, fold in the roasted mushrooms.

Begin adding the cream, 1/2 cup at a time and begin tasting. When ready, rice should be close to tender, but with a little more firmness to the bite. It should be slightly loose, with a creamy consistency.

Never overcook to a mush Remove pan from the heat and fold in the remaining butter and Parmesan cheese. Allow the risotto to rest for a couple of minutes.

Filet Mignon

Filet Mignon

7 ounces beef tenderloin
2 ounces maple BBQ glaze
1/4 ounces Arugula
1/4 ounces extra-virgin olive oil
To taste salt
To taste pepper

BBQ Sauce

1/4 cup canola oil

1 cup yellow onion, medium dice

1/3 cup sliced shallots

1 tablespoon mince garlic

3/4 cup cider vinegar

2 cups maple syrup

1 1/2 quarts Bull's Eye BBQ Sauce

2 ounces butter

1 sprig of rosemary

1 sprig of thyme

In a medium sauce pan, placed over medium high heat, add the canola oil.

Sauté the onion, shallots and garlic until it starts to brown and get caramelized.

Be careful not to burn. Add the maple syrup, BBQ sauce and whole butter.

Wrap the rosemary and thyme in cheesecloth and place in the pan.

Mix very well and allow to simmer for 1 hour.

Remove from heat and pull out the sachet. Squeeze the herbs with tongs to extract the flavor.

Mix the sauce until it is as smooth as possible. Adjust the seasoning and cool.

Store in airtight container. Dip the beef tenderloin in the olive oil.

Grill the beef tenderloin to your liking. Place 2 ounces of BBQ sauce on top.

Salt and pepper to taste.

Cream Cheese Mashed Potatoes

Yield: 8 portions

2 pounds Idaho potatoes, peeled

1 stick unsalted butter

8 ounces cream cheese

1 cup warmed milk

1 tablespoon kosher salt

black pepper to taste

Boil or steam potatoes until tender.

Using a food mill or mixer, incorporate all ingredients and adjust seasonings as necessary.

Cheddar Cheese Soup

1/2 lbs. bacon cut into 1/2 inch pieces
3 celery ribs cut into 1/4 inch pieces
3 cups milk
1 medium red onion cut into 1/4 inch pieces
2 tablespoons butter
3 cups water
3 dashes Tabasco
1 cup flour
1/2 cup beer
3/4 pound grated white cheddar cheese
salt and pepper to taste

In a soup pot start to brown the bacon over medium heat.
When the bacon is starting to get crisp, add the onions, celery and butter.
Cook until the onion is translucent.
Add the flour and incorporate with the butter.
Cook for 4 minutes, constantly stirring. Add the water and whisk.
Make sure there are no lumps.
Bring to a boil then reduce to a simmer and cook for 15 minutes, stir every couple of minutes.
Add the milk and continue to simmer for 15 minutes. Do not boil after you add the milk.
After the last 15 minutes, turn off the heat and stir in the cheese then the beer.
Add the Tabasco and season with salt and pepper.
If the soup is too thick you can thin it out with some milk.
Serve with your favorite bread and top with some chopped scallions or chives.

Maple Crème Brulee

Yield: 8 portions

1 pint heavy cream
6 ounces whole milk
1 1/2 cups granulated sugar
15 eggs egg yolks
2 teaspoons maple extract

Heat heavy cream, whole milk and granulated sugar over double boiler until sugar is dissolved (110F).

DO NOT WHIP.

Stir only. Place in a large mixing bowl.

Slowly add 1/3 of cream mixture to egg yolks, stirring to temper egg yolks.

Add remaining cream mixture. Stir to blend well.

Add maple extract to previous mixture. Strain mixture through fine mesh strainer.

Pour mixture into serving dishes that have been place into two cake pans.

Add enough water in the bottom of each cake pan to fill 1/4 the way up the serving dishes.

Bake in a low oven—275 degrees—for about 2 to 2 1/2 hours.

The desserts should be "set" firm but not hard, with a little wiggle when you shake it gently.

Sprinkle cooled custards with sugar and melt with a torch.

Cheddar Cheese Pretzel Bread

Makes 1 loaf (20 servings)

This giant twist is for those who are fans of soft pretzels. Rather than shaping the dough into individual portions, it is rolled in a thick rope and formed into one oversized knot.
Slice and serve with sausages and a good cold beer.

1/2 cup chopped onion

1 tablespoon butter or margarine

4-5 cups all-purpose flour

1 package active dry yeast

1 egg

2 cups shredded sharp cheddar cheese

1 1/4 cups warm water (*120-130 degrees*)

1 tablespoons sugar

1 1/2 teaspoons dried Italian seasoning, crushed

1/2 teaspoon salt

1 slightly beaten egg white

1 tablespoon water

1 teaspoon coarse salt (*optional*)

In a small skillet cook onion in hot butter or margarine till tender but not brown, about 7 minutes. Set aside to cool slightly.

In a large mixing bowl stir together 1 1/2 cups of the flour and the yeast. Add cooked onion, egg, cheese, 1 1/4 cups warm water, sugar, Italian seasoning, and salt. Beat with an electric mixer on low speed for 30 seconds, scraping bowl constantly.

Beat on high speed for 3 minutes.

Using a wooden spoon, stir in as much of the remaining flour as you can.

Turn dough out onto a lightly floured surface.

Knead in enough of the remaining flour to make moderately stiff dough that is smooth and elastic (*6-8 minutes total*).

Shape into a ball. Place in a lightly greased bowl; turn once.
Cover and let rise in a warm place till double (*1 to 1 1/4 hours*).
Punch dough down. Turn out onto a lightly floured surface and let
rest for 10 minutes.
Lightly grease a baking sheet. Roll dough into a 48-inch-long rope.
On the baking sheet form the rope into a large pretzel shape by
crossing one end over the other to form a circle, overlapping about
12 inches from each end.
Take one end in each hand and twist once at the point where the
dough overlaps.
Lift each end across to the edge of the circle opposite.
Moisten the ends and tuck underneath; press to seal.
Cover and let rise in a warm place till nearly double (*about 45
minutes*).
Stir together egg white and 1 tablespoon water; brush onto bread.
If desired, sprinkle lightly with coarse salt.
Bake in a preheated 375 degree oven for 40 to 45 minutes or till
bread is golden brown and sound hollow when tapped.
If necessary, cover loosely with foil the last 20 minutes of baking to
prevent over browning.
Remove from pan; cool completely on a wire rack.

Butterscotch Bread Pudding

Yield: 12 servings
1 1/16 pound Texas Toast
1 1/2 cups milk
2 1/2 cups eggs
1/2 cup condensed milk, sweetened
3 tablespoons orange juice
3/4 teaspoon salt
3/4 teaspoon nutmeg
1 1/2 tablespoons fresh vanilla
Cut bread into cubes. Mix the wet ingredients and spices together.
Soak bread in wet mixture for about 1 hour.
Fill ramekins 1/2 full with bread mixture.
Place butterscotch candy in the center ad fill up with more bread.
Bake for 20 to 25 minutes at 285 degrees.

Beef Barley Soup

Yield: 8 servings

2/3 pound onion, diced medium

2/3 pound celery, diced medium

5 1/3 ounces carrot, diced medium

5 1/3 ounces leeks, sliced 1/2 inch thick

2 2/3 ounces butter

2 ounces roasted garlic puree

1 1/3 quart beef stock, broth or low sodium bouillon

1 pound prime rib chunks, medium dice

1/3 ounce kosher salt

1/3 ounce black pepper

2 teaspoons dried oregano

2 teaspoons dried basil

1/3 teaspoon crushed red pepper

5 1/3 ounces precooked barley

2 fl ounces red wine

In a large sauce pot, heat the butter until fully melted. Add the onion, celery, carrot, and leeks and sauté until tender, about 6 to 7 minutes over medium heat.

Add the red wine and scrape the bottom of the pot, and reduce the wine by 3/4.

Add the beef stock, puree of roasted garlic, meat and spices. Cook together for 1 1/2 hours or until the flavors have blended together.

Add the pre-cooked barley.

Asian Shrimp Cocktail Plate

Yield: 6 servings

1 medium peeled carrot, julienned
1/2 red onion, julienned
1/2 cup julienned napa cabbage
1/2 red bell pepper, julienned
1 teaspoon freshly chopped cilantro, plus 6 whole stems for garnish
1 1/2 pound poached shrimp (*see note*)
1/4 cup horseradish chili sauce (*see note*)
3 tablespoons wasabi dressing (*see note*)
kosher salt to taste
finely ground black pepper to taste
6 (16 oz.) Asian style to-go boxes

Combine carrots, onions, cabbage, bell pepper, chopped cilantro, salt, pepper and 3 tablespoons wasabi dressing in a bowl.
Toss until all vegetables are coated with dressing.
Mix shrimp and half of horseradish chili sauce. Divide wasabi slaw among boxes.
Lean boxes on sides onto plates. Divide shrimp to place over slaw.
Spoon remaining chili sauce on plates. Drape box with a whole cilantro stem.

Wasabi Dressing

1 tablespoon sugar
1/4 cup rice wine vinegar
1 1/2 tablespoons dry wasabi powder
2/3 cup mayonnaise
salt & pepper to taste
Dissolve sugar in rice-wine vinegar.
Mix in dry wasabi powder until mixture becomes a thick paste.
Whisk in mayonnaise until smooth. There should be no lumps.
Season with salt and pepper.

Horseradish Chili Sauce

2/3 cup cold ketchup
1 teaspoon prepared horseradish
4 drops Tabasco sauce
4 drops Worcestershire sauce
1/4 lemon, juice only
salt & pepper to taste
2/3 cup Asian chili Sauce
Mix cold ketchup, prepared horseradish, Tabasco, 4 drops
Worcestershire and lemon juice.
Season with salt & pepper.
Mix 2/3 cup of ketchup mixture with 2/3 cup Asian chili sauce.
Season with salt & pepper.

Poached Shrimp

1 gallon water
2 tablespoons kosher salt
2 tablespoons Tabasco sauce
2 lemons, juice only
1 teaspoon crushed red pepper flakes
1 teaspoon black peppercorns
1 1/2 pound shrimp, (48-52 count)

Mix water, kosher salt, Tabasco and lemon juice in pot. Place crushed red pepper flakes and black peppercorns in coffee filter. Tie with string to secure. Add to water. Boil. Add peeled, deveined (*tail-off*) shrimp.

Cook 5 to 7 minutes or until shrimp turns pink and curls tightly. Remove shrimp.

Chill in freezer until cold. Refrigerate until ready to serve.